FLORENCE HENDERSON'S
*S*HORT-CUT COOKING

FLORENCE HENDERSON'S

SHORT-CUT COOKING

AMERICA'S FAVORITE MOM HELPS YOU GET DINNER ON THE TABLE FAST

Photography by Lisa Koenig

WILLIAM MORROW AND COMPANY, INC. / NEW YORK

It is the policy of William Morrow and Company, Inc., and its imprints and affiliates, recognizing the importance of preserving what has been written, to print the books we publish on acid-free paper, and we exert our best efforts to that end.

Library of Congress Cataloging-in-Publication Data
Henderson, Florence.
    Florence Henderson's short-cut cooking : America's favorite mom helps you get dinner on the table fast / Florence Henderson ; photography by Lisa Koenig. — 1st ed.
        p.   cm.
    Includes index.
    ISBN 0-688-16377-7
    1. Quick and easy cookery.   I. Title.
TX833.5.H46   1998
641.5'5—5dc21   98-38889
                                                                CIP
Food styling by Karen Pickus / Prop styling by Janet Bowblis

Printed in the United States of America

First Edition

1 2 3 4 5 6 7 8 9 10

BOOK DESIGN BY ANN GOLD

www.williammorrow.com

CONTENTS

CONTENTS

To my husband, John, who is still my recipe for happiness;

to my four children who survived all my learning attempts

at cooking and parenting, to become four of the most

wonderful human beings I know; and to Mady Land and

Allen Reid for their loyalty, support, and "know-how"

—qualities that have led to a long and fruitful

working relationship and lasting friendship

ACKNOWLEDGMENTS

With special thanks to Justin Schwartz at William Morrow and Company, for his editorial guidance; to Mady Land and Allen Reid, who created the idea for this book and who produced the public television series; to everyone at CPTV in Connecticut; and to the many wonderful people whose efforts and talents made this project happen, especially to Teresa B. Blackburn for her imaginative assistance with recipe development and testing, as well as her stylist's eye for presentation, and to Elizabeth Shenk for her food expertise and recipe development; and grateful appreciation to David Heaner and Damp Rid for being so supportive of this project.

FOREWORD

Like a lot of busy people who are always on the go, I've been a working "mom" balancing the demands of a family and a busy career. So, I've always looked for ways to save time, money, and stress, especially at mealtime. I believe in the idea of homemade, and I didn't want to give up taste or nutrition, even though it was often tempting to go out for fast food instead of preparing dinner myself. When dining out, I never know exactly what we are getting in our food, things like salt, fat, and sugar.

Unlike my character on *The Brady Bunch,* I didn't have an Alice to help me out! Particularly during those *Brady Bunch* years, out of necessity, I developed cooking short-cuts and strategies to feed my family with a minimum of time and fuss. Actually, I've worked hard in the kitchen since I was a young child growing up in southern Indiana, and had some great role models in my family.

I think mine is a pretty unique family. For instance, my father was forty-seven years old when he married my mother. That was his first and only marriage, and he had ten children! I was the tenth, born when my father was sixty-seven. I love to tell people this because I think it's so encouraging and really proves the saying "It's never too late."

We were very poor—short on money, but long on love and mutual support. As country kids who learned to fend for themselves at an early age, we were all taught to be independent and learned to cook because both my parents worked. I first learned to cook when I joined a 4-H Club. I baked a devil's food cake that won me a trip to the state fair in Indianapolis. It was a very special event and an encouraging reward for my effort in the kitchen.

My first "job" was when I was only eight, helping to take care of my oldest sister Pauline's baby and cleaning her house. Since she's always been an incredible cook and very organized in the kitchen, she was a great influence on my "culinary development." To this day, she can create wonderful, tasty food out of almost nothing. My parents, too, were both wonderful cooks. Since we didn't have much money, they made pretty basic dishes, but I can still taste my dad's vegetable soup, which he made from scratch, and my mother's garden salad, which she could whip up faster than anyone I know.

I worked my way through high school living with families, cooking, cleaning, doing laundry, and taking care of their children. It was very hard work, but I learned a lot about "household management" and never forgot.

My favorite job in high school was food related—working at Kent's Bright Spot, a soda fountain and bus station combined. I was a "whiz" behind that fountain, but to be honest, I gave away a lot of ice cream and also probably ate more than my share. Then, right out of high school, I went to New York. I was sponsored to study at the American Academy of Dramatic Arts, and I got my first professional job after my first year at the academy. I've been working ever since!

When I was first on Broadway, I learned to make healthy meals quickly because I was doing eight shows a week, studying voice, and acting in my spare time. I married very young and had my first child when I was twenty-one, and have always worked throughout my pregnancies. I didn't have as many as my mother, but I do have four wonderful children! So I always had to think ahead and plan meals.

In addition to the influences of my family and of professional necessity, another great source of kitchen savvy came from the eight years I hosted a cooking show on The Nashville Network called *Country Kitchen*. Each week, a guest brought a favorite recipe to share with our audience, and with the support of a terrific production staff, we researched and developed a tremendous file of great food tips and recipe facts. Many hints from those shows and guests are now part of my ever-growing storehouse of information.

These days, my grown-up children are on their own, but I have a new challenge. My husband, John, and I live on a boat in California, which has forced me to be creative about serving meals at home. With limited space for storage and room for fewer appliances, I've had to be very creative about food on board. "Double duty" is a very important concept under these conditions!

In *Short-Cut Cooking*, it's my pleasure to share with you some of the tips and recipes I've collected, and also to tell you about a few that my friends have shared with me. Have fun and keep on cooking!

FLORENCE HENDERSON'S
*S*HORT-CUT COOKING

$\mathcal{I}$NTRODUCTION

This collection of more than a hundred delicious, quick, and easy-to-prepare recipes and short-cuts come from my own experiences, as well as from my family and friends. The recipes can be used for all kinds of occasions and the preparation time for most averages only ten to fifteen minutes, depending on how quickly you work. A few recipes call for longer actual cooking times, but you can do other things while you wait for them to come out of the oven. You'll find that most use a minimum of fat, and that there are substitutes for almost any ingredient. I believe in improvising!

ABOUT THE TIPS

Wherever there's a particularly relevant time- or labor-saving hint, a short-cut tip appears next to or below the recipe. These are identified as to whether they are:

1. Serving Tips
2. Ingredient Savvy
3. Substitutions
4. Measurement Savvy
5. Plan Ahead
6. Recipe Rescue

7. Time Savers

8. Step Savers

9. Tool Tip

10. Sanity Saver

11. Mess Saver

12. Shopping Tips

13. Storage Tips

14. Gadget Substitution

15. Household Hints

16. Minis: These are extra "recipettes" or combinations of just a few ingredients, to be used as alternatives or to create interesting accompaniments such as sauces or dressings.

I often specify "fat-free" as optional for items like chicken broth, when I know that taste is not affected and the item is easily available. Although these recipes aren't "dietetic," I prefer to keep the fat content down whenever possible. However, if you prefer or if it's what you have on hand, you can certainly use the regular (full-fat) ingredient.

An ingredient I frequently use is balsamic vinegar, the fabulous Italian vinegar made from white Trebbiano grapes which gets its dark color and sweetness from aging in barrels. Store the vinegar in a cool, dark place, and it will keep for about six months after it's opened. I wouldn't suggest using plain red wine vinegar as a substitute, because it doesn't have the wonderful depth of flavor. However, if you don't have any balsamic vinegar on hand, here's a recipette or "mini":

½ cup red wine vinegar

2 teaspoons soy sauce (or tamari)

2 tablespoons honey

In a jar with a tight-fitting lid, shake all the ingredients together well. This mixture can be used immediately in recipes instead of balsamic vinegar, or can be stored in the refrigerator for up to one month.

You'll see quite a few recipes which call for "lemon or lime juice" because I think using citrus is a wonderful, healthy, and low-calorie way to perk up a dish. If you have the fresh fruits, they're worth the few minutes it takes to prepare them. But most recipes are just fine with bottled juice, so don't hesitate to substitute it for the fresh.

Several recipes include alcoholic ingredients like wine, brandy, rum, liqueur, or tequila, which you may prefer to skip. In each case, I've suggested an approximate substitute so you can enjoy the dish with as close to the original taste as possible. Experiment with fruit juices and nectars, such as peach, pear, papaya, and black currant; presweetened lime juice; or coconut milk.

Before you start cooking, organize your ingredients and utensils so you'll know if you're missing anything, and be sure to read the recipe all the way through to make sure there are no surprises.

But, even before you look at a recipe, I think there are several basic ways to help gain control over mealtime:

TO SAVE TIME, TAKE ADVANTAGE OF CONVENIENCE AND PREPARED FOODS

I prefer to use fresh ingredients whenever possible, but if time is short, by all means, use canned, bottled and frozen items. Many of these substitutions for fresh ingredients are so good that only the most discerning professional chef would be aware of the switch!

Today, supermarkets and groceries throughout the country provide a wide variety of ready-to-serve, "just heat up" ingredients like seafood, poultry, meat, and breads. There are also precut, prewashed salad ingredients like my favorite baby carrots, which are bite-sized, peeled, and ready to eat. Bottled salad dressings, pasta sauces, and canned soups save a lot of work, and can be made into many other quick and easy sauces and gravies.

These prepared ingredients can be used in all the recipes in this book which call for fresh. Your budget may not allow you to do this on a regular basis, since prepared food is usually more expensive. So make the most of these purchases by recycling leftovers into the next meal or by combining them with other dishes.

ORGANIZE YOUR KITCHEN SPACE, CLEAR THE COUNTERTOPS, AND EQUIP YOUR KITCHEN WITH THE BASICS

You can't waste time hunting for basic tools, or for a place to put down a bag. You need plenty of counter space and quick access to frequently used items. Make good use of drawers and, for spaces under sinks and in lower cabinets, buy inexpensive stacking shelves and add pull-out sliders. Consolidate long-handled utensils you use frequently and store them in a tall container. Put infrequently used items at the back of cabinets. Save space with some equipment that can do double duty, such as a blender for a food processor and a large, heavy skillet that can be used as a wok.

Make sure you have most of the following, and add items to this list as you find you need them:

UTENSILS AND TOOLS

Bottle and can openers

Colander (a strainer that stands on its own)

Corkscrew

Cutting board (wooden ones are better for your knives)

Kitchen scissors

Knives—the big three: chef's, paring (3-inch), and serrated (10-inch)

Measuring cups and spoons

Mixing bowls (stainless steel nesting is best)

Pastry cutter

Peeler (carrot/vegetable)—large rubber handle is best

Strainer

POTS AND PANS

Baking dish (2-quart glass or ceramic)

Cookie sheet (nonstick if possible)

Roasting pan with rack

Saucepans—small (2-quart) and medium (5-quart), with lids

Skillet—10- to 12-inch (nonstick if possible)

Stockpot (large, 8-quart)

OTHER VERY USEFUL GADGETS

Four-sided grater

Ice cream scoop

Instant-read meat thermometer

Ladle

Muffin tin

Pastry brush

Rubber spatula

Slotted spoon

Whisk

EQUIPMENT

Electric mixer (handheld is fine)

Food processor or blender

Microwave oven

Small coffee bean grinder

STAPLES TO STOCK UP ON

Aluminum foil

Coffee filters

Paper napkins

Paper towels

Parchment paper

Plastic wrap

Plastic bags (and trash bags)

Plastic storage containers (various sizes and shapes)

Resealable plastic bags in assorted sizes

Skewers (and wooden or bamboo chopsticks from takeout)

Wire ties

Wax paper

SUPPLIES AND CLEANERS TO KEEP ON HAND

Hand and dish soap

Dishwasher detergent

Sink and oven cleaners

Sponges

Rubber gloves

Dish towels

Pot holders

Matches

Band-Aids!

STOCK YOUR PANTRY WITH ESSENTIAL INGREDIENTS

If your shopping time is limited, make a list like the one below and invest time in one big expedition. Then track what needs replenishing by keeping a list in the kitchen and noting when ingredients are running low.

THE CUPBOARD

All-purpose flour

Baking powder

Baking soda

Canned chickpeas

Canned stocks, broths, and assorted soups

Canned tomatoes, Italian-style plum tomatoes, and tomato paste

Chocolate chips

Dried pastas—assorted

Jams and jellies—assorted

Maple syrup

Marinated artichoke hearts (jar)

Mustards—assorted

Nuts and seeds—assorted

Oils: olive (extra-virgin for uncooked, pure for frying) and vegetable

Peanut butter

Raisins

Rice—assorted

Roasted red peppers (jar)

Soy sauce

Spices—all: from curry to paprika

Sugar—brown and white

Vinegars—balsamic and other assorted

Good red and white wine, and assorted liqueurs

THE REFRIGERATOR

Bacon

Butter

Carrots

Celery

Eggs (large)

Fresh herbs and garlic

Cheese blocks—Cheddar, Parmesan, Romano, Monterey Jack, and
  mozzarella

Ketchup

Mayonnaise

Milk

THE FREEZER

Fruit juice concentrates (orange, grapefruit, etc.)

Chicken breasts—skinless and boneless

Coffee and coffee beans

Frozen fruits and berries—raspberries, strawberries, blueberries, and
  peaches

Frozen vegetables—spinach, corn, peas, and beans

Premium vanilla ice cream

Sourdough bread

THE FRUIT AND VEGETABLE BINS

Apples, pears, bananas—assorted fruits

Garlic

Onions

Potatoes

Lemons, or bottled lemon juice

SHOPPING AND STORING STRATEGIES

If your shopping list shows that your "balances" are low, it's time to make a deposit! Try to predict the most convenient, stressless time to shop, when the stores are least crowded and you have fewer other deadlines. And try not to go when you're hungry and can't resist many unnecessary temptations! Use the same stores frequently become familiar with the layouts and find the right aisles and product locations quickly. Get to know the personnel so they can help you with special requests. Try to buy frozen and refrigerated items last so they won't spoil or defrost in the shopping cart, and put fragile items like fruit and vegetables on top of heavier bottles and cans.

Buying larger sizes can often save money, but only if you have storage space and are sure the food will be used before it spoils and gets thrown away. Try to plan meals according to perishability of items, using fresh first, then frozen, canned, and packaged later.

Remember that once they're opened, some items such as mayonnaise or ketchup need to be moved from the pantry to the refrigerator. Try to store herbs and spices in a drawer away from light and heat. This extends their expiration dates, and it's easier to find individual containers when they're not stacked on top of or behind each other in a cabinet. Label everything in the freezer with dates and descriptions so you'll remember what's in there!

In general, if you substitute prepared ingredients for fresh, and improvise by replacing items you don't have on hand with those in your pantry, you'll be able to prepare meals quickly. Measuring by "eye" can speed up the process too. Exact measurements aren't critical except perhaps for serious baking. For instance, just squeeze lemons for an approximate amount of juice—and don't worry about spoonfuls.

When possible, buy thin cuts or small pieces of meat, fish, and poultry, or spend a few minutes cutting them up prior to cooking because the smaller the food, the faster it cooks. The quickest cooking methods are grilling, broiling, sautéing, and stir-frying.

And when all else fails, the very last resort is the telephone and a take-out menu! Or, as my friend Joan Rivers says, "What do I make for dinner? Reservations!"

SIMPLIFIED WEIGHTS AND MEASURES

dash = less than ⅛ teaspoon

3 teaspoons = 1 tablespoon

1 tablespoon = ½ fluid ounce

16 tablespoons = 1 cup

1 cup = 8 fluid ounces

1 cup = ½ pint

2 cups = 1 pint

2 pints (4 cups) = 1 quart

4 quarts (liquid) = 1 gallon

8 quarts (solid) = 1 peck

4 pecks = 1 bushel

16 ounces = 1 pound

BUTTER MEASUREMENTS

2 cups = 4 sticks = 1 pound

1 cup = 2 sticks = ½ pound

½ cup = 1 stick = ¼ pound

¼ cup = ½ stick = 4 tablespoons

PART-CUPS BY TABLESPOON

4 tablespoons = ¼ cup

5⅓ tablespoons = ⅓ cup

8 tablespoons = ½ cup

10⅔ tablespoons = ⅔ cup

12 tablespoons = ¾ cup

14 tablespoons = ⅞ cup

OVEN TEMPERATURES

Warm = 270° to 300°F

Moderate = 325° to 350°F

Fairly hot = 375° to 400°F

Hot = 425° to 450°F

Very hot = 475° to 500°F

CAN CONTENTS

8 ounces—1 cup

No. 300—1¾ cups

No. 1 Tall—2 cups

No. 303—2 cups

No. 2—2½ cups

No. 2½—3½ cups

No. 3—4 cups

No. 10—12 to 13 cups

**MAXIMUM FREEZER STORAGE
TIMES AT 0°**

Butter—6 to 8 months

Ice cream—2 months

*Frozen vegetables, commercially
prepared:*

Asparagus—8 to 12 months

Green beans—8 to 12 months

Corn—8 to 10 months

Spinach—14 to 16 months

Fish, raw:

Fish, fatty—6 to 8 months

Fish, lean—10 to 12 months

Poultry, raw:

Chicken—12 months

Duck—6 months

Turkey—12 months

Meat, raw:

Beef—6 to 12 months

Ground beef—3 to 4 months

Lamb—6 to 9 months

Ground lamb—3 to 4 months

Pork—3 to 6 months

Ground pork—1 to 3 months

Bacon—1 month

Smoked ham—2 months

Veal—6 to 9 months

Ground veal—3 to 4 months

Wild game—9 months

STARTERS, SNACKS, ACCESSORIES

When your life is hectic and you need to entertain family and friends without much time for planning, it's important to have a few standby recipes for appetizers and snacks. I've relied on my dear friend Jim Nabors as a great source of ideas. After his series, *Gomer Pyle,* Jim bought a beautiful ranch on Maui, in Hawaii, where he grows macadamia nuts. We all know how addictive they are! I now use nuts of all kinds in a wide range of dishes in addition to snacks.

Some of these recipes were suggested by friends and guests on my cooking show, *Country Kitchen.* They range from dumplings to chicken wings, and all have become favorites of mine. Other recipes are inspired by my love of all foods Italian, like crostini, bruschetta, and focaccia. The one thing all of these recipes have in common is that they're simple, fast, and make use of basic ingredients you're likely to keep in your pantry.

Read your recipe all the way through, and always preassemble your recipe ingredients and utensils before you begin to cook. If you organize everything in order of use, you won't leave anything out while you work. It's hard to keep track of where you are in a recipe if you have to stop to hunt for things in between steps! Premeasure ingredients whenever possible so everything is ready to go, and you'll save even more time once you start!

SUN-DRIED TOMATO BITES

For impulse entertaining, I try to have ingredients on hand to make what I call "little bites." These instant appetizers are easy to prepare, easy to eat with one hand, and appeal to guests who are "just grazing" or just want a "nibble." The sun-dried tomato has a nice intense flavor, so you don't need much of it. I love capers too, and even if you're not sure about using them, I think you'll love the taste of them in this recipe!

MAKES 10 TO 12 SERVINGS

1 cup finely chopped sun-dried tomatoes (packed in oil)

1 teaspoon minced garlic

1 cup olive oil, preferably extra-virgin

1 small jar capers, rinsed and drained

1 to 2 loaves of crusty French bread, sliced into ½-inch-thick slices

½ cup grated Asiago cheese

1. In a medium-large bowl, mix together the sun-dried tomatoes, garlic, and olive oil. Stir the capers into the mixture.

2. Spread the bread slices out on a flat surface. Drizzle about a tablespoon of the sun-dried tomato mixture over each slice of bread. Using the back of a spoon, lightly press the mixture into the surface of each slice and let it soak in.

3. Scatter some of the cheese over each of the slices of bread and serve.

SHORT-CUT TIPS

PLAN AHEAD: You can make these a few hours ahead. Spread the prepared slices out flat on a cookie sheet, and cover with foil or plastic wrap until ready to serve. The bread will soak up even more of the mixture. Delicious!

RECIPE RESCUE: To rehydrate the kind of sun-dried tomatoes that aren't packed in oil, let them stand in a bowl of hot water for about 30 minutes. Drain before using, and save the flavored water for soups and sauces.

TIME SAVER: Hard cheese is easier to grate or shred at room temperature than when it's cold. To shred easily and quickly, use a food processor. Clean-up will be easy if you spray the blades or grating disk with nonstick vegetable spray prior to use.

ZESTY HOT NUTS

Like most people who travel frequently by airplane, I've sampled many a snack of mixed nuts. Most people seem to love them as much as I do, so I thought I'd serve a spiced-up version of them at home too. My sister Ilean and her husband, Ed, send us a huge tin of mixed nuts every year, which Ed hulls himself, and the almonds are my favorite. Putting together this appetizer couldn't be simpler if you buy the ingredients in packages. The recipe has no set amounts—just use what looks right for the number of guests you expect. These are great with cocktails, especially margaritas, which are another specialty of mine—according to my guests!

Pesto sauce (premade from supermarket)

Whole almonds

Whole cashews

Whole peanuts

Pecan halves

Walnut halves

(Any other nuts you like: hazelnuts, macadamia nuts, etc.)

Ground cayenne pepper

1. In a nonstick skillet over medium-high heat, add enough pesto sauce to coat all of the nuts and stir.

2. Add the nuts to the pesto sauce, and toss in the skillet until all the nuts are thoroughly coated, about 1 minute.

3. Remove the skillet from the heat and sprinkle the cayenne pepper to taste over the nuts. Cool the nuts on paper towels spread out on a flat surface. Serve in small bowls, strategically located throughout your entertaining areas.

SHORT-CUT TIPS

SUBSTITUTION: If you don't have cayenne pepper, use very finely crushed red pepper flakes.

STEP SAVER: To chop nuts, place on a cutting board. With a chef's knife, using a rocking motion, chop nuts to desired size. If you have a large quantity to chop for a recipe, place the nuts in a food processor and pulse quickly.

STORAGE TIP: The oil content of most nuts makes them subject to spoilage and they can become rancid quickly. Store nuts, shelled or unshelled, in a dry, cool place. They can be stored up to about 6 months if refrigerated, and up to a year in the freezer.

TOMATO-CUCUMBER COCKTAILS

Although these cocktails look very elegant, using a blender or a food processor cuts preparation time down to almost nothing. They're great to serve when you are having wings, since these cocktails have a wonderful spicy flavor. You can serve them as a "real" cocktail by adding vodka, or just enjoy the nonalcoholic version, which is very healthy. I frequent health food stores and am always amazed at the mixtures they use for their vegetable and fruit drinks. I think mine is delicious!

MAKES 8 SERVINGS

One 28-ounce can whole tomatoes with liquid

4 cucumbers, peeled, seeded, and cut into chunks

2 carrots, cut into chunks

½ *each* green, red, and yellow bell pepper, seeded and cut into chunks

½ medium red onion, chopped

2 tablespoons balsamic vinegar

2 tablespoons red wine vinegar

1 tablespoon olive oil, preferably extra-virgin

Hot pepper sauce

Salt and freshly ground black pepper

Optional: chilled vodka to add as desired

Garnish: celery sticks (julienne-cut, about 4 inches long); lemon and lime wheels (see Serving Tip)

> **MINI:**
>
> QUICK AND EASY CHEESE TOAST: **Slice some crusty French bread and place it on a baking sheet. Top each slice with a mixture of goat cheese and shredded Cheddar cheese. Place in a 350°F oven until the cheese is bubbly and melted.**

1. Place the tomatoes, cucumbers, carrots, bell peppers, and onion into a food processor fitted with a metal blade, and pulse until almost smooth.

2. Empty the mixture into a glass or nonreactive bowl and stir in the vinegars, olive oil, hot pepper sauce, and the salt and black pepper to taste. Mix well. Chill the mixture for about 30 minutes before your guests arrive.

3. To serve, pour the cocktail mixture into small wineglasses or plastic cups, then garnish with celery sticks and lemon or lime wheels. The mixture is thick, so provide spoons, and serve with Quick and Easy Cheese Toast (recipe on page 17).

---

*S*HORT-CUT TIPS

SERVING TIP: To make the citrus wheel garnish, cut a lemon or lime into thin slices. Then, with a small sharp knife, slit one slice halfway through to the center, and position (slip) it onto the rim of the glass. Combine the lime and lemon slices to make the garnish more colorful.

SANITY SAVER: If your celery has tough stems, just "peel" the string from the ribs with a knife before using, or grab the bottom inch or so, bend it, and pull! Tough celery stalks can actually be hard to eat.

QUICK AND EASY DUMPLINGS

Dumplings are a change of pace for last-minute entertaining. Some of us think of them as just a country dish, like the recipe Loretta Lynn made on my cooking show, Country Kitchen. *Since dumplings are a Henderson family specialty, I'm somewhat partial to them. But after sampling the Asian variety, I started experimenting with different wrappers and fillings. This assortment of dumplings makes an impressive buffet, which can be made ahead and kept frozen for last-minute guests. Serve the dumplings with a variety of bottled or jarred sauces to make it extra quick!*

MAKES 10 TO 12 SERVINGS

SPINACH-RICOTTA FILLING

¾ cup ricotta cheese

½ cup chopped fresh spinach

1 teaspoon minced garlic

¼ cup freshly grated Parmesan cheese

Salt and freshly ground black pepper

BLACK BEAN–CORN FILLING

One 15.5-ounce can black beans, rinsed, drained, and mashed

½ cup ricotta cheese

⅓ cup frozen corn kernels, thawed and well drained

½ teaspoon hot pepper sauce

1 teaspoon ground cumin

Salt and freshly ground black pepper

DUMPLING WRAPPERS

2 packages won ton skins (about 30 wrappers each)

1 teaspoon cornstarch mixed with 2 tablespoons water

Vegetable oil for cooking dumplings

1. To make the spinach-ricotta filling, in a glass bowl, mix together the ricotta cheese, spinach, garlic, and Parmesan cheese. Season with salt and pepper to taste. Chill the filling before using.

2. To make the black bean–corn filling, in another glass bowl, mix together the beans, ricotta cheese, corn, hot pepper sauce, cumin, and salt and black pepper to taste. Chill the filling before using.

3. To fill and cook the dumplings: Spread the won ton wrappers out on a flat surface. Stir the cornstarch-water mixture. Place a rounded teaspoon of filling in the center of each wrapper. With your fingers, wet the edges of each wrapper with the cornstarch-water mixture. Fold the won ton wrapper in half over the filling and pinch the edges together to form a "packet," keeping the filling in the center and the edges sealed. Repeat with the remaining wrappers, using up all the filling. Store any leftover wrappers in the refrigerator in a plastic bag. Cook all the filled dumplings now or freeze some to cook later.

4. In a large nonstick skillet, heat 3 tablespoons of oil over high heat until the oil is hot enough to really sizzle. Reduce the heat to medium-high. Place the dumplings in the skillet in a circular pattern, pinched side up and not touching, to form a single layer. Cook until the bottoms of the dumplings are golden, 2 to 3 minutes. Reduce the heat to medium.

5. Gently pour into the pan about ½ to 1 cup of water (depending on the size of the pan). Cover the pan. Steam the dumplings for 5 to 6 minutes. Uncover the pan and let the water cook off. As batches of dumplings are cooked, transfer them to a serving platter, with the golden brown sides up, and cover lightly with aluminum foil. Place in a warm oven until ready to serve.

SERVING SUGGESTION: Have bowls of good-quality jarred tomato sauces and/or pesto to serve with the spinach dumplings. Try some unusual salsas to serve with the black bean dumplings, like mango or red pepper salsa.

SHORT-CUT TIPS

SUBSTITUTION: In a pinch, use well-drained cottage cheese instead of ricotta. Drain it in a paper towel–lined sieve over the sink for about 30 minutes, then puree.

STEP SAVER: Although frying adds flavor, skip this step and omit the oil if you're looking to lower the fat content. Just steam these dumplings in a bamboo steamer set over a pot of boiling water.

TOOL TIP: Use a pastry cutter or even a fork to quickly mash beans.

SANITY SAVER: For a fun way to carry around extra cooking utensils, wear a tool belt, which is sturdy and has many pockets. Leave your hands free and save trips to locate what you need.

HOUSEHOLD HINT: To clean brass or copper quickly when you're getting ready to entertain, make a paste of lemon juice and salt and enough flour to make it thick. Apply like a commercial paste with a rag or paper towel, rubbing gently, then rinse well.

THREE-WAY CHICKEN WINGS

When Pittsburgh Steeler "Mean Joe" Greene showed up on Country Kitchen *with his Texas Wings, they turned out to be an audience favorite, and I filed away the recipe for use at home. Over time, I made up new versions of his barbecue sauce–based dish using lighter ingredients and grilling instead of baking to save time. My husband, John, loves anything barbecue, so he really thinks I'm an angel when I make these wings!*

MAKES 3 DOZEN WINGS

FIRST-WAY WINGS

4 whole scallions, chopped

½ cup apricot preserves

1 tablespoon minced fresh ginger

¼ cup olive oil, preferably extra-virgin

Juice of 1 lime

Salt and freshly ground black pepper

Dash of cayenne pepper

12 chicken wings, rinsed and patted dry

1. Preheat the grill or broiler.

2. In a glass or nonreactive bowl, stir together the scallions, preserves, ginger, olive oil, and lime juice. Add the salt and pepper and the cayenne to taste.

3. With a pastry brush, coat the wings with this mixture.

4. Grill or broil the wings, turning occasionally and brushing on more preserve mixture, until they're thoroughly cooked and crispy, about 5 to 6 minutes on each side. Serve hot or at room temperature.

SECOND-WAY WINGS

½ cup lemon juice

4 bay leaves

2 tablespoons dried rosemary leaves

1 tablespoon dried thyme leaves

4 cloves garlic, minced

1 teaspoon hot pepper sauce

Salt and freshly ground black pepper

12 chicken wings, rinsed and patted dry

1. In a mixing bowl, stir together the lemon juice, bay leaves, rosemary, thyme, garlic, and hot pepper sauce. Add salt and pepper to taste.

2. Add the wings to the bowl and toss to coat well. Let marinate for about 30 minutes in the refrigerator, stirring occasionally.

3. While the wings are marinating, preheat a grill or broiler. Grill or broil the wings, basting with leftover marinade, until completely browned and thoroughly cooked, about 5 to 6 minutes on each side. Serve hot or at room temperature.

THIRD-WAY WINGS

½ cup tamari or soy sauce

¼ cup molasses

¼ cup ketchup

3 cloves garlic, minced

1 teaspoon crushed red pepper flakes

¼ cup orange juice

2 tablespoons peanut oil

12 chicken wings, rinsed and dried

1. Preheat the grill or broiler.

2. In a glass or nonreactive bowl, mix together the tamari sauce, molasses, ketchup, garlic, hot pepper flakes, orange juice, and peanut oil.

3. Brush the molasses mixture over the wings to coat well. Grill or broil the wings, basting with the molasses mixture, until they're crispy brown and thoroughly cooked, about 5 to 6 minutes on each side. Serve them hot or at room temperature.

---

*S*HORT-CUT TIPS

SANITY SAVER: Molasses, like honey and maple syrup, has a stronger flavor the darker it is.

MESS SAVER: Before measuring, lightly coat the measuring utensil with vegetable oil so that the molasses slides right off instead of sticking.

BASIC BRUSCHETTA

This is a wonderful "feast in a flash" appetizer, and a staple of Italian cuisine. For variation, add some grated Asiago or Romano cheese, fresh herbs, or chopped pine nuts. Another popular version which I like adds finely chopped tomatoes. Experiment and enjoy. Almost anything works if you enjoy the resulting taste!

MAKES 4 SERVINGS

8 slices of crusty, country bread, cut about 1 inch thick

4 large cloves garlic, peeled, cut in half, and crushed

Olive oil, preferably extra-virgin

Salt and coarsely ground black pepper

1. Toast the bread on both sides until golden brown and well toasted on the outside, and softer on the inside.

2. Rub one side of each slice of toast with a garlic half. Press the garlic lightly into the surface. The garlic will be absorbed into the bread.

3. Place the bread on a serving platter and drizzle each slice with olive oil. Add salt and pepper to taste. Allow the flavors and the oil to soak into the bread for about 5 minutes and then serve.

SHORT-CUT TIPS

INGREDIENT SAVVY: Extra-virgin olive oil is considered the finest and fruitiest of olive oils, with the deeper color and more intense olive flavor. Light olive oil has less color and fragrance, and a rather nondescript taste. It has a higher smoke point than other olive oils, so it can be used for high-heat frying, unlike other olive oils.

SUBSTITUTION: Try using some of the available delicious flavored olive oils for this recipe. You can buy olive oil with basil or rosemary added, as well as hot pepper or garlic.

CROSTINI

When you serve your guests crostini, a wonderful sampling of Italian ingredients, they can create their own appetizers if you serve the toppings in separate bowls. Keep a supply of these ingredients in your kitchen so you'll always be able to whip them up. For instance, Italian or baguette bread slices can be stored in the freezer for months, and you don't even need to thaw them before you toast the slices! Plan on 2 to 3 crostini per guest, then multiply to come up with the number of bread slices you need. It's a good idea to preslice your bread before you freeze it.

MAKES 6 TO 8 SERVINGS

24 slices of French bread (best if less than
    ½ inch thick), toasted

Olive oil, preferably extra-virgin

Chopped fresh herbs: a mixture of basil,
    thyme, oregano, and parsley

Roasted garlic (see Ingredient Savvy opposite)

8 ounces cream cheese, softened

Italian spice blend (from your spice rack, or
    see Mini)

Chopped sun-dried tomatoes (packed in oil)

Black olive paste (buy in large supermarkets
    or international grocery stores—or see
    page 209)

Roasted red bell peppers (sold in jars), sliced

Premade pesto sauce

MINI:

ITALIAN SPICE BLEND: **If you don't have any on hand, make your own. In a coffee grinder, place 1 tablespoon dried rosemary leaves, and grind until fine. Add 2 teaspoons ground sage, 3 tablespoons dried oregano, and 3 tablespoons dried basil. Grind quickly just to mix. Store seasonings in an empty, airtight spice bottle, away from heat and light.**

1. Spread out all of the toast slices on a flat surface.

2. Drizzle some slices with olive oil and top with the fresh herbs and roasted garlic.

3. Spread some slices with cream cheese. Sprinkle on the spice blend and sun-dried tomatoes.

4. Smear the black olive paste on other slices, then top with roasted red bell slices.

5. Spread the remaining slices with pesto.

6. All crostini can be served either at room temperature or warmed slightly.

SHORT-CUT TIPS

INGREDIENT SAVVY: To roast garlic, gently rub the outer layers of papery skin off a head of garlic and separate into cloves. Place the cloves on a square of aluminum foil large enough to loosely enclose them. Drizzle with 1 teaspoon olive oil, then wrap and seal. Bake at 400°F for 25 to 30 minutes, or until they're soft when pierced with a knife tip. (You can roast the entire head without separating it into cloves, although it won't become slightly caramelized as do the individual cloves.) The cloves will open easily and the softened garlic can be used as a spread like butter, or as an ingredient as called for in recipes.

HOUSEHOLD HINT: To clean a coffee grinder that has been used to grind other flavorings, without scrubbing and rinsing in the sink, just grind up a few pieces of plain bread, then shake it out. The bread absorbs all traces of the odors and flavors.

SUN-DRIED TOMATO, BASIL, AND ONION FOCACCIA

This flat Italian bread is like a mini pizza, which has a sprinkling of many different herbs, cheese, or pesto. I like to serve my friends this one, which has plenty of pizzazz!

**MAKES 8 SERVINGS AS AN APPETIZER
OR ACCOMPANIMENT**

Olive oil

Pizza dough (frozen or refrigerated kind from the supermarket), enough for one 12-inch pizza

6 to 8 sun-dried tomatoes (packed in oil), chopped

¼ cup chopped fresh basil, or 1 tablespoon dried

1 medium yellow onion, finely chopped

¼ cup grated Romano cheese (or use Parmesan)

1 clove garlic, minced

Freshly ground black pepper

1. Preheat the oven to 425°F. Lightly drizzle a baking sheet with the olive oil. Set it aside.

2. On a lightly floured surface, roll or press out the dough into a rectangle about 10 by 14 inches. Place the dough on the baking sheet.

3. Scatter the chopped sun-dried tomatoes over the dough. Sprinkle the basil, onion, and Romano cheese evenly over the dough.

4. Scatter the garlic over all. Add pepper to taste.

5. Lightly press the ingredients into the surface of the dough. Picking up one of the short sides of the dough rectangle, fold it in half. It will now be a rectangle approximately 10 by 7 inches. Pat or roll it out to about 10 by 10 inches.

6. Place in the oven and bake until the crust is golden brown, about 20 minutes. Slide the focaccia onto a wire rack and cool for about 5 minutes.

7. Cut it into small squares to serve as an appetizer or into wedges to serve as an accompaniment to soup or salad.

SHORT-CUT TIPS

RECIPE RESCUE: If using dry-packed sun-dried tomatoes, you can quickly soften them by placing the dried tomatoes in a glass bowl with warm water, wine, or juice. Let the tomatoes sit for about 10 minutes, then drain and chop.

MESS SAVER: Cut sun-dried tomatoes with scissors to reduce clean-up time. Cut fresh basil with scissors directly onto the pizza as well.

FOUR-CHEESE
BUTTERMILK BISCUITS

I have Willie Nelson to thank for inspiring me to get back to biscuits. When Willie prepared a cream gravy for a hearty country breakfast on Country Kitchen, *he reminded me how much I loved biscuits when I was growing up. They're easy and always seem to say "welcome home." This is a recipe you'll always be prepared to make if you keep some of this mix on hand. I think it's a pleasant surprise when served an appetizer or snack. Getting to sing with Willie was pretty inspirational too!*

MAKES ENOUGH FOR 6 TO 7 BATCHES OF BISCUITS

12 cups all-purpose flour

6 tablespoons baking powder

7 teaspoons salt

1 generous tablespoon freshly ground

black pepper

1 generous tablespoon paprika

½ cup unsalted butter, chilled and cut

into chunks

½ cup vegetable shortening, chilled

½ cup grated sharp Cheddar cheese

½ cup grated Gruyère cheese (or Swiss

or Jarlsberg)

¼ cup grated Romano cheese

¼ cup grated mozzarella cheese

TO MAKE 1 RECIPE OF BISCUITS

2 cups biscuit mix

1 cup buttermilk

MINI:

SWEET CHEESE BISCUIT
MIXTURE: **You can easily
create a new flavor by
adding some brown sugar
and chopped dried fruit
to the mix. To create
Herb Biscuits, add dried
herbs to the basic cheese
mixture.**

FUN KIDS' BISCUITS:
**Children love animal or
other shaped biscuits, so
using cookie cutters, cut
the dough into shapes
such as bears, stars, or
cars. Even better, let the
kids get involved and
press out their own
biscuits.**

1. To make the mix, in a large bowl, combine
well the flour, baking powder, salt, pepper, and paprika.

2. Add the chilled butter chunks and vegetable shortening to the mixture.
Using a pastry cutter, cut the butter and shortening into the flour.

3. Add the cheeses. Using a pastry cutter, cut the cheese into the dough.
The mixture should be crumbly with no large chunks. If not ready to
use, store the mixture in an airtight container in the refrigerator. This
will keep for about 3 to 4 weeks. You can also store it in a freezer for
months!

4. Preheat the oven to 475°F.

5. To make one batch of biscuits, place 2 cups of the cheese biscuit mix in a bowl. Make a "well" in the center of the mixture. Pour the buttermilk into the "well." Combine the mixture with a fork until the mixture is just blended. Do not overmix.

6. On a lightly floured surface, gently pat the dough out to about ½ inch thick. Cut the biscuits with a biscuit or cookie cutter. Use all the scraps. Place the biscuits on an ungreased cookie sheet.

7. Bake the biscuits in the oven until golden brown, 10 to 12 minutes. Serve warm.

*S*HORT-CUT TIPS

MEASUREMENT SAVVY: One cup of grated Romano cheese equals ¼ pound (4 ounces).

PLAN AHEAD: Measure the biscuit mix out into recipe portions (2 cups), wrap well, and freeze. Remove individual batches from the refrigerator as needed.

RECIPE RESCUE: To rescue dried-out bread, bagels, or biscuits, place a damp paper towel or napkin around them and microwave for about a minute.

STEP SAVER: Buy premixed biscuit mixes from the supermarket and add cheeses.

GADGET SUBSTITUTION: A pastry cutter makes it easy to prepare biscuit dough. If you don't have one, try using two knives. Cut the knives through the dough mixture in a crisscross fashion, with the blades facing inward. This method isn't as easy, but the final result is the same.

BANANA-CARROT MUFFINS

These lovely light muffins are a great addition to a Sunday breakfast when you want something sweet to go with your coffee—that's actually the time I enjoy sweets the most! It's worth the extra time to make up a batch and freeze it to have on hand. These muffins are great at teatime, to take on a picnic, to bring as a house gift, or to pack into a lunchbox or snack pack for you or your kids.

MAKES 12 SERVINGS

½ cup unsalted butter, softened

¾ cup sugar

2 large eggs

1 cup mashed ripe bananas
    (approximately 2 medium)

⅓ cup milk

2 teaspoons vanilla extract

½ cup shredded carrot

2 cups all-purpose flour

½ cup chopped pecans

1 teaspoon baking soda

½ teaspoon salt

> **MINI:**
>
> CINNAMON HONEY CREAM CHEESE: **It's easy to make this spread for warm muffins. Combine one 8-ounce package of softened cream cheese, 2 tablespoons honey, and 1 teaspoon ground cinnamon. Mix until creamy.**

1. Preheat the oven to 350°F.

2. In a large bowl, cream together the butter and sugar with a large spoon until the mixture is light and fluffy. Beat in the eggs. Stir in the mashed bananas, milk, and vanilla. Add the shredded carrot and stir just until blended.

3. In another bowl, stir together the flour, pecans, baking soda, and salt.

4. Add the flour mixture to the butter mixture and stir just until blended and the dry ingredients are just moistened.

5. Spoon the mixture into regular muffin tins lined with paper or foil liners, or use nonstick muffin tins. Bake in the oven for 35 to 45 minutes, or until a toothpick inserted in the middle of each muffin comes out clean. Serve warm.

M I N I :

ENGLISH MUFFIN HALVES:

Toast English muffin halves well and add a bit of margarine or butter. Spread with cottage cheese, top with some applesauce, then sprinkle with cinnamon.

SHORT-CUT TIPS

SERVING TIP: Keep your muffins warm for longer by lining your bread basket with aluminum foil, then a napkin or cloth.

SANITY SAVER: To test baking soda, which can deteriorate with age, combine ¼ teaspoon baking soda with 2 teaspoons vinegar. If the mixture bubbles, the baking soda is active and still usable.

STEP SAVER: If you don't have muffin-tin liners, to get nicely rounded muffins, grease the muffin cup only halfway up the sides. If it's coated too high up, the batter will pour over the top and the muffins may stick.

STORAGE TIP: Bananas can be held at the just-ripe stage by storing them in the refrigerator. Although the peel will discolor, the banana will be ripe for about another six days. Mashed banana pulp can also be frozen.

FRESH TUNA CREPES

Here's a lightweight recipe to serve for a sophisticated crowd. Although this recipe sounds elegant, it requires little time or effort to put together. You can make these well ahead and serve them cold. And they're convenient for buffets, since they can be eaten like an ice cream cone or hot dog, and so require little clean-up!

MAKES 6 SERVINGS

2 tablespoons canola or vegetable oil

½ small onion, chopped

2 cloves garlic, chopped

One 4.5-ounce can green chiles, chopped

One 14.5-ounce can diced tomatoes, drained

Salt and freshly ground black pepper

1 pound fresh tuna, grilled or broiled until cooked through and
　　　broken into chunks

1 package premade crepes (12)

1. In a skillet over medium-high heat, heat the oil. Add the onion and garlic and cook until the onions are translucent, 2 to 3 minutes.

2. Stir in the chiles and tomatoes. Heat thoroughly, 1 to 2 minutes. Season to taste with salt and pepper. Remove the skillet from the heat.

3. Stir in the cooked tuna until it's well mixed.

4. Wrap the crepes in foil and warm them in a 300°F oven.

5. Cut the warm crepes in half. Fill each half with some of the tuna mixture and roll it up like a "cone."

6. Place the filled crepes on a baking sheet, cover loosely with a sheet of aluminum foil, and set aside until ready to serve. Refrigerate if serving later or next day, but serve at room temperature. To serve, place the crepes on a decorative serving platter.

---

*S*HORT-CUT TIPS

SERVING TIP: Drizzle the crepes with a premade béarnaise or hollandaise sauce.

SANITY SAVER: When grilling fish, choose fillets or steaks no more than about 1 inch thick, or the exterior can char before the interior is done.

    To keep fish from sticking to the grill, first brush the grill lightly with vegetable oil, or spray it with nonstick cooking spray.

EGGPLANT AND ROASTED RED BELL PEPPER DIP

I've always found dips addictive, but I'm on the lookout for "calorie villains"! This recipe is the result of my search to create a weight-friendly dip that's tasty and healthy, yet quick and easy to prepare. It's wonderful to serve at parties. I'm also addicted to unsalted tortilla chips with any kind of dip, and they're great with this one!

MAKES 4 TO 6 SERVINGS

2 tablespoons olive oil

1 medium onion, chopped

One 1- to 1½-pound eggplant, diced

2 roasted red bell peppers (jarred is fine), chopped

2 tablespoons lemon juice

Salt and freshly ground black pepper

⅓ cup chopped fresh basil leaves

2 tablespoons chopped fresh parsley

2 ripe tomatoes, diced

1. In a heavy skillet over medium heat, heat the olive oil and cook the onion until it becomes softened and translucent, 2 to 3 minutes.

2. Add the eggplant, roasted bell peppers, lemon juice, and salt and black pepper to taste. Cook, stirring, until the eggplant has softened, 8 to 10 minutes. Cover and continue to cook for about 5 minutes more.

3. Remove the skillet from the heat. Stir in the basil, parsley, and chopped tomatoes.

SERVING SUGGESTIONS: Serve with toasted French bread, Melba toast, crudités, or tortilla chips.

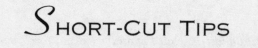

SHORT-CUT TIPS

MEASUREMENT SAVVY: One pound of eggplant equals 3 to 4 cups chopped.

RECIPE RESCUE: To prevent the eggplant flesh from discoloring after it's cut, brush it with lemon juice, or dip it in a quart of water mixed with 3 tablespoons of lemon juice.

SALADS

My mother was the salad maker in my family, with a lot of wisdom to impart to the ten of us kids! Her garden salad included everything grown in our garden, chopped up and tossed with her country version of a vinaigrette—the dressing from Heaven! To this day, my sister Ilean and her husband, Ed, who live in Tell City, Indiana, grow, freeze, and can their own food. But my favorite short-cut learned from my mother is "how to participate in a democracy through salad making." You leave all the ingredients out on a counter and let everyone build their own salad. They work and you rest! Boy, did my mother need a rest with us all going in ten directions!

There's nothing like a salad for versatility, and you don't have to be on a diet to enjoy a hearty dinner salad. These recipes range from the most basic fresh greens, to nourishing salad entrées based on beans, beef, fish, fruits, potatoes, and pasta. They're refreshing in hot weather and great as traditional light starters or as a way to combine and use up leftovers.

Invest in a few inexpensive plastic squeeze bottles of various sizes to store dressings and other sauces. You can create the dressing right in the bottle, without dirtying bowls. Then use it to easily drizzle exact amounts into mixtures or on top of salads or other dishes. Make sure to label the bottles and keep them in the refrigerator for future use.

FRESH GREEN SALAD
WITH BASIC VINAIGRETTE

This recipe couldn't be simpler since you just assemble the basic salad and vinaigrette, then add ingredients to suit your own palate. Use whatever fresh greens you have, whether from your own garden or your local market. For texture and crunch, add bell pepper strips, broccoli florets, shredded cabbage, mushrooms, slices of apples or pears, orange wedges, or steamed asparagus. To perk up the vinaigrette, add balsamic vinegar, toasted chopped pine nuts, fresh herbs, whole-grain or Dijon mustard, Parmesan cheese, and anything else you like. The possibilities are endless!

MAKES 6 SERVINGS

6 to 8 cups of greens, torn into bite-sized pieces (use one variety or a
combination)
4 scallions, minced (white part only)
¼ cup white wine vinegar
¼ cup white wine (or white grape juice)
⅓ cup olive oil, preferably extra-virgin
Salt and freshly ground black pepper

1. Place the greens in a large salad bowl or serving platter.

2. In a small bowl, whisk together the scallions, vinegar, wine, oil, and the salt and pepper to taste. Whisk until emulsified. Adjust the seasonings to taste.

3. Drizzle the dressing over the salad greens and toss gently. Use just enough dressing to coat the greens lightly, but don't soak. Serve the salad immediately.

4. Put any leftover dressing in a jar with a tight-fitting lid and refrigerate until your next salad. You can shake it up right in the jar.

*S*HORT-CUT TIPS

SUBSTITUTIONS: Other greens to use are mesclun salad mix, red or green cabbage, watercress, and/or spinach.

PLAN AHEAD: To transport a green salad (to a party or a picnic), make the salad directly in a plastic container with a vacuum seal. First, pour in the dressing, then place the greens on top, but don't toss the ingredients together. Close the lid tightly. When it's time to eat, shake the container gently, yet firmly enough to toss the salad and mix it with the dressing. There's no mess, no utensils, and it's ready to serve. You can toss your salads at home this way too.

STORAGE TIP: To keep greens fresh for 4 to 5 days, wash and pat them dry. Wrap loosely in paper towels and place in a plastic bag, stored in the refrigerator until ready to use.

MIXED GREENS GREEK SALAD WITH CREAMY FETA DRESSING

This dish features the wonderful Kalamata olive, named for the region in Greece where it's grown. My husband's parents, who lived in a small town there, brought their family recipes with them when they settled in Chicago. Whenever I make this dish, I thank them and remember the time we enjoyed it at an outdoor tavern at the foot of the Acropolis, celebrating the hundredth anniversary of the Olympics in 1996. While we sat there, some locals recognized me from The Brady Bunch, *and I realized what a small world it really is!*

MAKES 4 SERVINGS

2 cups mesclun salad greens (or larger greens torn into bite-sized pieces)

1 large ripe tomato, cut into thin wedges

½ medium red onion, cut into thin slivers

½ medium green bell pepper, cored, seeded, and cut into thin slivers

⅓ cup Greek Kalamata olives

Creamy Feta Dressing (recipe opposite)

MINI:

ROSEMARY OLIVES: **Drain a jar or can of Kalamata olives and place them in a glass jar. Add a few stems of fresh rosemary, tucked in and around the olives. Fill the jar with olive oil. Add a pinch of crushed red peppers and 2 cloves garlic. Close the lid of the jar and store in refrigerator for about 2 weeks. The olive oil will turn cloudy, but will become clear at room temperature. Remove the jar from the refrigerator about 30 minutes before serving. The olives become infused with the garlic and rosemary. Delicious!**

1. Place the salad greens in a large serving bowl. Sprinkle the tomato, red onion, bell pepper, and olives over the greens. Cover with damp paper towels and chill before serving.

2. To serve, remove the bowl from the refrigerator and drizzle the greens with the desired amount of Creamy Feta Dressing. Toss.

---

*S*HORT-CUT TIPS

SUBSTITUTIONS: A variety of great olives to use in this salad:

Spanish—green stuffed type

Black or Mission—ripe green olive

French Niçoise—tiny dark brown brine cured and then packed in oil

Dry Cured—packed in salt, which removes most of their moisture, creating dry, wrinkled fruit

PLAN AHEAD: To create your own olive mixtures by the pound, visit the salad bar or takeout bar of your supermarket. Most large supermarkets now carry a good selection of imported olives. These are usually much fresher tasting than those in jars or cans, and cost less.

CREAMY FETA DRESSING

Feta, a classic Greek cheese, is traditionally made from goat's or sheep's milk and has a very rich, tangy, salty taste. Today it's often made from cow's milk. It's a white, crumbly, and rindless cheese, usually pressed into square cakes. Since it's salty, taste your recipe first before adding table salt to dishes that have feta cheese in them.

⅓ cup olive oil, preferably extra-virgin

3 tablespoons lemon juice

2 cloves garlic, minced

2 teaspoons dried oregano

⅓ cup crumbled feta cheese

Salt and freshly ground black pepper

1. Pour the olive oil and lemon juice into a blender or a food processor bowl.

2. Add the garlic, oregano, feta cheese, and salt and pepper to taste. Blend them until smooth.

3. Adjust the seasonings to taste. Pour the dressing into a jar with a tight-fitting lid and refrigerate it until ready to use.

4. Bring the dressing to room temperature and shake the jar well before using the dressing on a salad.

SHORT-CUT TIPS

SUBSTITUTIONS: For very special salad dressings, try the flavored feta cheeses found in the cheese department of the grocery, like feta with sun-dried tomatoes and basil, or feta with cracked pepper and garlic.

TIME SAVER: To use feta cheese, simply crumble a bit at a time and add to recipes. You can also purchase feta that is already crumbled.

STORAGE TIP: Since feta is a crumbly cheese, the texture changes very little when frozen. Wrap excess feta tightly in freezer wrap and place it in a sealable plastic bag. It can be frozen for up to 2 months. Because feta contains water, thaw it in the refrigerator before using so that it retains its firm texture.

RED LEAF LETTUCE, APPLE, AND WALNUT SALAD

Here's one of those no-time, no-work salads with little to clean up. I love the contrast of flavors and textures of the apple chunks, walnuts, lettuce, and dressing. What a delicious way to get your "apple a day"!

MAKES 4 SERVINGS

2 tablespoons red wine vinegar

2 tablespoons olive oil

1 teaspoon Dijon-style mustard

1 teaspoon honey

1 clove garlic, minced

1 scallion, minced

Salt and freshly ground black pepper

1 bunch red leaf lettuce, rinsed and patted dry

1 tart red apple, cored and chopped

¼ cup toasted, chopped walnuts (see Ingredient Savvy, page 44)

MINIS:

Create wonderful specialty mustards using a basic Dijon-style mustard as the base.

Dill Mustard: In a bowl, combine ½ cup chopped fresh dill, 2 cups Dijon mustard, 2 tablespoons sour cream, 3 long pieces of lemon rind, and the juice of ½ lemon. Whisk together well. Pour the mixture into a glass jar or jars. Seal with tight-fitting lids and store in the refrigerator. Keeps for up to 1 month.

Tarragon-Shallot Mustard: In a bowl, combine ½ cup chopped tarragon leaves, ¼ cup minced shallots, 2 cups Dijon mustard, and 1 tablespoon balsamic vinegar. Mix well. Pour the mixture into a glass jar or jars. Seal with a tight-fitting lid and refrigerate. Keeps for up to 1 month.

1. Pour the red wine vinegar and olive oil into the bottom of a salad bowl. Whisk together well.

2. Add the mustard and honey and whisk again.

3. Add the garlic, scallion, and salt and pepper and whisk again.

4. Tear the lettuce greens into bite-sized pieces, adding them to the bowl as you tear.

5. Scatter the apple and the walnuts over the top. If serving immediately, toss the salad. If not, cover with damp paper towels and refrigerate until ready to serve.

SHORT-CUT TIPS

INGREDIENT SAVVY: To add crunch and intensify the flavor of nuts, toast them before using them in a recipe. Place the nuts in an ungreased pan or skillet over medium heat, and cook, stirring frequently, until they're golden brown. Nuts can also be toasted in a 350°F oven, stirred occasionally, for 10 to 15 minutes.

If you prefer to use a microwave, place 1 cup chopped nuts on a paper plate and microwave them on high, uncovered, for 3 to 4 minutes, or until they smell toasted. They won't change color as much as if toasted by other methods, although they will taste toasted. Be sure to wait until they're cool to taste them.

RECIPE RESCUE: To prevent apples from turning brown after you've cut them, put the slices in a bowl of ice water with citrus juice. Lemon juice will make apples tart, orange juice makes them sweeter.

SANITY SAVER: If you first coat your measuring spoon lightly with oil, the honey will slide right off.

HEARTY HOPPIN' JOHN SALAD

This recipe is based on a traditional Southern dish served on New Year's Day. It features black-eyed peas, one of the least expensive and most nutritious beans you can buy, and is very good either as an entrée or side dish. If used as an entrée, serve it with some great bread.

MAKES 4 SERVINGS

1½ cups ham strips, cut julienne-style (cooked deli ham, country ham, or Virginia)

3 cups cooked canned or frozen black-eyed peas (use dried peas cooked according to package directions)

1 package white and wild rice mix (Uncle Ben's type), cooked according to package directions

½ red bell pepper, cut into julienne strips

½ green bell pepper, cut into julienne strips

3 whole scallions, thinly sliced

1 carrot, very thinly sliced

Salt and freshly ground black pepper

¼ cup vegetable oil

¼ cup olive oil

¼ cup balsamic vinegar

2 tablespoons honey

2 tablespoons Dijon-style mustard

1 teaspoon dried Italian seasoning

Bibb lettuce leaves

> **M I N I :**
> CREATE AN EASY HONEY
> MUSTARD TO HAVE ON
> HAND FOR SALAD
> DRESSINGS: **In a bowl,
> whisk together 1 cup
> Dijon mustard and 1/2
> cup honey. Store until
> ready to use in a jar with a
> tight-fitting lid.**

MINI:

RED WINE–WHOLE-GRAIN
MUSTARD: **In a bowl, soak
¼ cup light mustard
seeds in 2 teaspoons
tarragon vinegar and 2
tablespoons red wine
overnight. Bring the
mixture to a boil in a
small saucepan over
medium-high heat and
add 1 cup Dijon mustard.
Let cool and store in a jar
with a tight-fitting lid.**

1. In a large mixing bowl, combine the ham, black-eyed peas, rice, red and green bell peppers, scallions, carrot, and salt and black pepper to taste. Toss together gently.

2. In a jar with a tight-fitting lid, combine the vegetable oil, olive oil, balsamic vinegar, honey, mustard, and Italian seasoning. Close the lid tightly and shake until the mixture is emulsified. Adjust the seasonings to taste.

3. Pour the dressing over the ham-peas-rice mixture and toss it gently to coat well.

4. To serve, cover the bottom of a plate with Bibb lettuce and place a serving on top.

*S*HORT-CUT TIPS

TIME SAVER: If using dried peas, sort through them and discard any bad peas. Rinse well and drain. When in a hurry, soak in warm water for about 15 minutes. Then proceed to cook as usual. This will speed up the process.

GOURMET-ON-THE-RUN SALAD

This salad is a perfect example of "using what you have on hand." If you keep your pantry stocked with items you use often, you'll always be able to whip up a recipe you enjoy. By adding good-quality ingredients to something more basic, you can create special dishes, like topping a baked potato with caviar! In fact, sometimes I make a baked potato with different toppings my whole lunch. In this recipe, the canned items would work equally well to zip up appetizers, sides, or entrées. Bottled dressing, the quickest way to top this salad, can also be used as a sauce or marinade for other dishes.

MAKES 4 SERVINGS

3 cups favorite greens (one variety or a mesclun mixture)

One 14-ounce can hearts of palm, rinsed, drained, and sliced

One 6.1-ounce can Mandarin oranges, drained

¼ cup chopped toasted nuts (almonds, pecans, hazelnuts, page 44)

A few whole raspberries, frozen or fresh

A bottle of your favorite honey mustard salad dressing

1. Prechill your salad plates in the refrigerator.
2. Place an equal amount of the salad greens on each salad plate.
3. Slice and scatter the hearts of palm over each plate.
4. Place some of the Mandarin oranges decoratively over each bed of greens.
5. Scatter the nuts over each.

6. Around the outer edge of each salad plate, place whole berries.

7. Drizzle the dressing lightly over all. Serve immediately.

SHORT-CUT TIPS

RECIPE RESCUE: If you're not serving a salad immediately, to prevent it from getting soggy, compose the salad and leave off the dressing. Lightly cover the greens with a damp paper towel. When ready to serve, add the dressing.

STORAGE TIP: "Quick freeze" whole berries when they're plentiful in the summer for use all year. Rinse and pat dry whole, ripe, fresh berries. Place in a single layer on a baking sheet and place uncovered in the freezer. When the berries are hard-frozen, place in plastic bags. The berries will be ready to use as needed, and can be stored for up to 4 months. Freezing berries in this way will keep them whole and separated when stored.

TOMATO, BASIL, AND FRESH MOZZARELLA SALAD

One of my favorite experiences in Italy (beside the art, museums, and eating) was sampling the fresh mozzarella, known here as buffalo mozzarella. Luckily, it's found in the United States in most large supermarkets, Italian markets, and cheese shops, so Americans can enjoy it too. There are very few ingredients in this recipe, so the quality of each is very significant. Try to use the best you can find!

MAKES 4 SERVINGS

2 large, ripe tomatoes, sliced ¼ inch thick (or cherry tomatoes, sliced)

½ pound fresh mozzarella cheese, thinly sliced

½ cup shredded fresh basil

Good-quality balsamic vinegar

Good-quality olive oil, preferably extra-virgin

Salt and freshly ground black pepper

1. Divide the tomato slices equally among the serving plates, arranging them in a decorative pattern.

2. Place the slices of fresh mozzarella in a decorative pattern on top of the tomatoes.

3. Scatter the shredded basil over all.

4. Drizzle each salad with the desired amount of vinegar and oil.

5. Add salt and pepper to taste. Serve immediately.

SHORT-CUT TIPS

INGREDIENT SAVVY: Mozzarella is a soft white Italian cheese with a mild, delicate flavor that is good in salads or sandwiches and makes a great snack with crackers or crusty bread. Packaged American mozzarella is drier and good for cooking. The best fresh mozzarella will be labeled "buffalo mozzarella," which means it's most likely from Italy, and was made from water buffalo's milk. It's now commonly made from cow's milk. Fresh mozzarella is usually sold in balls and packed in whey or brine. When you buy it, pour off the whey, rinse if desired, then slice. This cheese is best used uncooked, to appreciate its wonderful texture.

SUBSTITUTION: In winter when it's hard to find flavorful large tomatoes, use cherry tomatoes in this salad. Place the slices of fresh mozzarella on the plate first, then top them with the smaller tomato slices.

STORAGE TIP: Store unripe tomatoes stem side down at room temperature. Don't place in sunlight. At temperatures over 85°F, tomatoes turn yellow instead of red, and too much sunlight causes the skin to shrivel. Once a tomato has been refrigerated, it won't ripen.

Caesar Salad with Tenderloin Strips

Who can resist a Caesar salad? Over the years, I've streamlined mine to create this snappy salad entrée, which combines salad and steak, and merely suggests the anchovies as an option for those who like them. I'm also sharing my recipe for a Caesar dressing that has no eggs.

Makes 4 to 6 servings

One 8-ounce tenderloin steak, grilled medium to medium rare (see Time Saver)

1 to 2 bunches romaine lettuce

⅓ cup freshly grated Parmesan cheese

1 cup garlic-flavored croutons (store-bought, or see Mini)

Freshly ground black pepper

CAESAR DRESSING

2 cloves garlic, crushed

2 anchovies (optional)

1 generous tablespoon Dijon-style mustard

1 tablespoon red wine vinegar

2 tablespoons lemon juice

2 teaspoons Worcestershire sauce

¼ cup olive oil, preferably extra-virgin

¼ cup vegetable oil

MINI:

GARLIC CROUTONS: **Cut a few slices of bread into small cubes. Rub the inside of a skillet with 1 clove of garlic. Add a tablespoon of olive oil and a tablespoon of butter and melt them together over medium-high heat. Add the bread cubes and cook until evenly crisp and golden, 3 to 4 minutes, tossing often while cooking. Drain on paper towels. Sprinkle with Parmesan cheese, if desired, before using.**

2 tablespoons freshly grated Parmesan cheese

Freshly ground black pepper to taste

1. Thinly slice the grilled tenderloin steak, cover, and set aside.

2. In a large salad bowl, tear the romaine lettuce into bite-sized pieces. Scatter the Parmesan cheese over the top of the lettuce.

3. Top the lettuce with the croutons and add pepper to taste. Cover the salad loosely with damp paper towels and refrigerate.

4. To make the dressing, in a jar with a tight-fitting lid, combine all the ingredients. Close the lid tightly and shake until the dressing is emulsified. Adjust the seasonings to taste.

5. To serve, drizzle the desired amount of dressing over the salad and toss lightly. The lettuce leaves should be coated but not soggy! Scatter the tenderloin strips over the salad and serve with extra dressing on the side.

SHORT-CUT TIPS

PLAN AHEAD: Place some of the dressing in the bottom of the salad bowl before adding the other ingredients. Cover and chill until ready to serve. Toss as usual. The dressing is ready at the bottom of the bowl with no soggy lettuce!

TIME SAVER: Since "thinner cooks quicker," cut the steak into strips that are 4 inches long by ¼ inch wide before cooking. Sear quickly in a skillet for about 3 to 4 minutes. Let cool for 5 to 10 minutes and add to salad.

SHOPPING TIP: Caesar salads in plastic bags are available in the produce section of many supermarkets for when you're in a big hurry or just want a salad for lunch. Some come complete with croutons and dressings!

Classic Salad Niçoise

This salad is a great entrée, especially when you want something light and fresh tasting. You can use a low- or no-fat bottled dressing if you're in a big hurry. My husband, John, likes the anchovies in this recipe so much, he has an extra serving on the side! But if you don't find them appealing, just leave them out. The salad is still delicious.

MAKES 6 SERVINGS

VINAIGRETTE

¼ cup tarragon vinegar or white wine vinegar

¼ cup balsamic vinegar

½ cup olive oil, preferably extra-virgin

1 teaspoon dried thyme

½ bunch fresh parsley, chopped

Salt and freshly ground black pepper

SALAD

12 new red potatoes

1 pound fresh thin green beans

Mini:

PERFECT HARD-COOKED EGGS: **Place the eggs in cold salted water in a saucepan. Place over high heat and bring to a boil. Immediately remove the pan from the heat and cover. Let the eggs sit in the water for 10 minutes. Remove the eggs and place in a bowl of ice water. Let them sit for about 15 minutes, then crack them gently and peel. Plunge the eggs into cold water periodically to loosen their shells even more.**

24 ounces canned albacore tuna, well drained (use fresh grilled if
     time permits)

6 whole eggs, cooked, peeled, and quartered lengthwise

6 whole ripe tomatoes, cored and cut into eighths

½ cup pitted whole black olives (niçoise or Kalamata)

10 anchovy fillets, rinsed and patted dry

1. To make the dressing, place the vinegars and olive oil in a jar with a
   tight-fitting lid. Close the lid tightly and shake the jar until the
   ingredients are emulsified. Add the thyme, parsley, and the salt and
   pepper to taste. Shake the mixture again until well mixed. Set aside.

2. To make the salad, in a large pot of boiling water, cook the potatoes
   until tender, 15 to 20 minutes. Drain well, let cool for 5 to 10 minutes,
   and cut each in half.

---

*S*HORT-CUT TIPS

RECIPE RESCUE: If you like anchovies but find them too salty, place
them in a colander and rinse under cold water. Pat dry and use in
recipes.

SANITY SAVER: To tell if an egg is hard-cooked or not, just spin it. If
it wobbles, it's uncooked. If it spins evenly, it's cooked! Next time,
remember to mark it with an ✗!

STORAGE TIP: Store eggs in their carton inside the refrigerator rather
than in the compartment in the refrigerator door. Each time you open
the door, the eggs are exposed directly to a temperature change which
may cause them to go bad at a faster rate.

3. Trim the beans. Place them in a microwave-safe bowl with about ¼ cup of water and steam them in the microwave until they're tender and crisp.

4. Flake the tuna into a bowl. Try to leave it as chunky as possible. Add half of the dressing to the tuna and toss lightly.

5. On a large serving platter, scoop the tuna mixture into the center, mounding it somewhat.

6. On the outside edge of the platter, alternate the egg quarters, new potatoes, and tomato pieces, creating a circular border.

7. In the area of the platter between the egg border and the tuna mound, scatter the green beans and olives.

8. Scatter the anchovy fillets randomly over the vegetables.

9. Drizzle the remaining vinaigrette over all. Serve immediately.

NOTE: If serving later, wait to drizzle the final dressing until ready to serve.

CANNELLINI BEAN SALAD

When I was growing up, pinto beans were a staple in our household because they're both filling and nutritious. I still enjoy them but have sampled many other beans, which I've added to my menus. This recipe features cannellini beans, the Italian white beans, which are good to use in salads because they're large and firm. You can buy them dried or in cans. This dish makes a good party salad or even a vegetarian entrée.

MAKES 4 TO 6 SERVINGS

Two 15-ounce cans cannellini (or Great Northern) beans, rinsed and
  drained

2 tablespoons minced red onion

½ red bell pepper, cut into thin strips

¼ cup sliced, pitted black olives

¼ cup chopped fresh parsley

1 teaspoon dried Italian seasoning

Juice of 1 lime

Splash of balsamic vinegar

2 tablespoons olive oil

Salt and freshly ground black pepper

1. Place the beans in a mixing bowl. Add the onion, bell pepper, black olives, and parsley. Toss together gently.

2. Over the mixture, sprinkle the Italian seasoning, lime juice, vinegar, and olive oil. Toss gently, but well.

3. Season to taste with the salt and pepper. Serve immediately, or cover and refrigerate before serving.

SHORT-CUT TIPS

STORAGE TIP: To keep parsley fresh, rinse and stand the sprigs in a glass or jar of water. Cover the tops loosely with a plastic bag, and keep in the refrigerator until ready to use. Another method is to rinse a bunch of fresh parsley in cool water, pat dry with paper towels, then wrap loosely in damp paper towels and store in a plastic bag.

Spinach, Pecan, and Smoked Salmon Salad with Orange-Dill Vinaigrette

This quick and elegant dish is a gift from my sister Ilean, who still grows her own vegetables. I wish I lived closer to her so I could get them more often. When they visit, she and her husband, Ed, always bring me fresh tomatoes, cucumbers, nuts, and their home-canned beets and bread-and-butter pickles. Although my ingredients are usually store-bought, this combination is a winning way to get your family to eat their spinach!

MAKES 4 SERVINGS

VINAIGRETTE

⅔ cup olive oil, preferably extra-virgin

¼ cup red wine vinegar mixed with 2 tablespoons balsamic vinegar

2 tablespoons orange juice

½ teaspoon finely grated fresh orange zest (no white pith)

2 teaspoons chopped fresh dill

Salt and freshly ground black pepper

SALAD

1 pound fresh spinach leaves, rinsed and dried

½ cup toasted pecan halves (page 44)

½ pound smoked salmon

½ red bell pepper, cored, seeded, and cut into thin strips

½ yellow bell pepper, cored, seeded and cut into thin strips

1. To make the vinaigrette, in a jar with a tight-fitting lid, combine the olive oil, vinegars, and orange juice. Shake until emulsified.

2. Open the jar and add the orange zest, dill, and salt and pepper to taste. Close again and shake the mixture well. Chill until ready to use.

3. To make the salad, place the spinach leaves in a large salad bowl or platter.

4. Scatter the pecan halves over the spinach leaves.

5. Crumble the chunks of salmon over the top of the spinach.

6. Add the strips of red and yellow bell peppers. Drizzle with the desired amount of dressing and toss gently to coat the spinach leaves.

SHORT-CUT TIPS

SUBSTITUTION: Add some endive, curly endive, or red leaf lettuce to this salad for added taste and texture.

MEASUREMENT SAVVY: One pound of spinach equals 10 to 12 cups of torn pieces, or about 1 cup cooked. One 10-ounce package of frozen spinach equals about 1½ cups.

PLAN AHEAD: For faster chilling of salads, keep the serving plates in the refrigerator until ready to use.

SANITY SAVERS: Since fresh spinach is very gritty, wash it thoroughly before storing or using. Pull the leaves off the stems, and put them in a large container or directly into a large bowl filled with cold water. With your hands, swish the leaves around so that the dirt falls to the bottom. Dry the leaves thoroughly by blotting them with paper towels or using a salad spinner.

To remove excess moisture from frozen spinach, hold it over a bowl and squeeze it. You can save the liquid for soups or other dishes. Or, to dry the leaves completely, wrap them in paper towels and twist gently until all the moisture is absorbed.

GADGET SUBSTITUTION: Use a vegetable peeler to remove the zest from oranges. You can do this quickly and avoid the pith.

SATURDAY LUNCH
WALDORF CHICKEN SALAD

This traditional salad lends itself to any number of variations according to what you have in your pantry: golden raisins, dried cherries or currants, jícama, pears, carrots, or onions would all be delicious. I think this dish makes a lovely no-fuss weekend lunch for family or guests. Again, experiment and enjoy!

MAKES 4 TO 6 SERVINGS

3 cups chopped, cooked chicken meat

½ cup chopped celery

½ cup chopped apples (use whatever variety is in season in your
　　supermarket)

½ cup seedless red or green grape halves

½ cup chopped salt-free cashews (or use pecans or walnuts)

Juice of 1 lemon

¼ cup sour cream (or fat-free yogurt)

½ cup regular or low-fat mayonnaise

1 tablespoon chopped fresh dill

Salt and freshly ground black pepper

Bibb lettuce leaves

1. Place the chicken meat in a mixing bowl.

2. Add the celery, apples, grape halves, and nuts. Toss together lightly.

3. Drizzle the lemon juice over the mixture.

4. Add the sour cream and mayonnaise and toss well. (Add a bit more of each if you like a moister salad mixture.)

5. Add the fresh dill and stir to combine. Add the salt and pepper to taste.

6. To serve, place the lettuce leaves on plates and top each serving with a mound of the chicken salad. Serve immediately or cover and chill for an hour before serving. Add a loaf of crusty bread and some wine for a fabulous lunch.

JÍCAMA AND CABBAGE SALAD WITH CITRUS-HONEY DRESSING

This salad is fun to eat because it's so crunchy! In fact, once the kids become familiar with jícama, and cabbage, they'll ask for second servings. Jícama, a large bulbous root vegetable looking somewhat like a potato, has a sweet, nutty flavor. It's good both raw and cooked, in salads, soups, and stews. Just peel it by pulling the thin brown skin off with a sharp knife. I also like to combine cabbage with chickpeas and a salad dressing of lemon juice, olive oil, low-fat mayonnaise, a pinch of sugar, and a few drops of Tabasco sauce. Formidable!

MAKES 6 SERVINGS

SALAD

1 small jícama (or half of a medium), peeled and cut into julienne
    strips

1 half small head green cabbage, shredded with sharp knife

1 medium red bell pepper, cored, seeded, and cut into 2-inch
    julienne strips

DRESSING

¼ cup olive oil, preferably extra-virgin

¼ cup orange juice

1 tablespoon lime juice

2 teaspoons honey

Salt and freshly ground black pepper to taste.

1. To make the salad, in a large bowl, combine the jícama, cabbage, and
   red bell pepper.

2. To make the dressing, in a small bowl, whisk together all the dressing
   ingredients. Pour the dressing over the salad, toss well, and chill until
   ready to serve.

SHORT-CUT TIPS

SUBSTITUTION: If you can't find jícama in your market, the closest
substitute in texture is water chestnuts.

MEASUREMENT SAVVY: One pound of jícama equals about 3 cups,
chopped.

TIME SAVER: To "julienne" is to cut foods into thin sticklike strips.
Crunchy vegetables such as the jícama and bell pepper used in this
recipe are great to cut this way.

SIMPLE POTATO SALAD

Irish potatoes were another staple of my childhood, and to this day, I love potatoes in any form. I can't think of another dish which is so universally enjoyed and served for so many kinds of occasions as potato salad. This recipe is super quick and perfect as part of a ready-to-go meal! Remember to look for potatoes that are firm and blemish free and nicely shaped. New (waxy) potatoes are a good choice, since they retain their shape after being cooked. A plus for nutrition, potatoes are high in potassium and vitamins C and B_6!

MAKES 4 TO 6 SERVINGS

2½ to 3 pounds potatoes, washed and unpeeled

2 tablespoons chopped scallion greens

½ cup sour cream

½ cup mayonnaise

2 tablespoons red wine vinegar

1 tablespoon lemon juice

2 tablespoons diced red bell pepper

1 teaspoon paprika

Salt and freshly ground black pepper

1. Bring a large pot of water to a boil and cook the potatoes 20 to 30 minutes, or until they're softened but not mushy. Remove the potatoes from the water and set aside to cool. Cut into bite-sized chunks.

2. In a salad or mixing bowl, stir together the scallion greens, sour cream, mayonnaise, vinegar, lemon juice, bell pepper, and paprika.

3. Add the potato chunks to the bowl and toss gently until the potatoes

are well coated. Add salt and pepper to taste. Serve the potato salad at room temperature or cover it and chill.

SHORT-CUT TIPS

SUBSTITUTION: If you don't have sour cream, use equal parts plain yogurt and cottage cheese. For this recipe use ¼ cup each. Put them in a blender or food processor and blend just until smooth.

MEASUREMENT SAVVY: One pound of new potatoes equals 8 to 10 potatoes.

TIME SAVER: When you have a few extra minutes and a whole bag of lemons, juice the lemons, then freeze the juice in ice cube trays. When frozen, pop out the cubes and put in plastic freezer bags. This way you'll always have fresh lemon juice on hand for recipes!

MESS SAVER: Quickly chop scallion greens into recipes by using scissors. Cut directly into the bowl. There's no surface to clean up.

STORAGE TIP: Store potatoes in a cool dry place and they'll keep for weeks. Don't store them near onions, which release a gas that hastens the spoilage of potatoes. And don't keep potatoes in the refrigerator—the starch will convert to natural sugar and the potatoes will become overly sweet and dark.

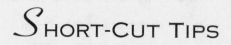

CRUNCHY COLESLAW

When a group of us were visiting friends and unexpectedly ended up staying to watch a game on TV, our hostess put together an unusual, impromptu indoor picnic. For example, she added pears and apples to a traditional coleslaw recipe to create a distinctive side dish. Popular pears such as Anjou, Bosc, Bartlett, and Comice are generally available year-round, although you can use any type of pear or apple for this recipe. The crunchy texture is great and not too sweet if you use a nice tart apple.

MAKES 4 SERVINGS

½ small head red cabbage, coarsely grated

2 carrots, coarsely grated

1 crisp pear, cored, seeded, and chopped

1 crisp, tart apple, cored, seeded, and chopped

1 rib celery, diced

¼ to ½ cup bottled coleslaw dressing

1. In a glass bowl, combine the cabbage, carrots, pear, apple, and celery. Toss well.
2. Drizzle the dressing over the vegetables and fruits, and toss until well coated. Cover the salad and chill until ready to use.

---

*S*HORT-CUT TIPS

RECIPE RESCUE: If cutting apples and pears ahead of time, soak the slices in a small amount of orange or lemon juice. Drain before adding to the recipe. The acid in the citrus juices keeps the fruit from turning brown, and using orange juice adds a nice sweet flavor to the recipe.

TIME SAVER: Packaged, preshredded cabbage and carrots are available in the produce section of most supermarkets today. Use these when every minute in the kitchen counts.

STORAGE TIP: Unlike most fruits, pears are ripe when they're still firm. You can ripen pears by putting them together with an apple in a paper bag that has been pierced in several places with a knife tip. The apple releases a gas that hastens the process.

GRAPEFRUIT AND AVOCADO SALAD WITH POPPY SEED DRESSING

This is a variation on one of my hot-weather favorites—an avocado filled with baby shrimp salad. The grapefruit is light and refreshing and, combined with the dressing, it's a wonderful blend of sweet and tangy flavors. The avocado has a buttery texture, and once it's been scooped out of its shell, you can use the shell as a container for serving salad or dips. Actually, you can do the same with your grapefruit—just make sure its skin is thick enough to hold your salad.

MAKES 6 SERVINGS

2 large ruby red grapefruits

2 ripe avocados

¼ cup balsamic vinegar

2 tablespoons orange juice

1 tablespoon honey

1 tablespoon poppy seeds

1. Peel and slice the grapefruit into sections. Remove the seeds.

2. Cut the avocados in half and remove the pit. Peel away the skin and slice.

3. Arrange the grapefruit and avocado slices decoratively on a serving platter.

4. In a bowl, whisk together the vinegar, orange juice, honey, and poppy seeds. Drizzle the dressing over the platter and serve.

SHORT-CUT TIPS

INGREDIENT SAVVY: You can intensify the flavor of poppy seeds by toasting them, either in a skillet over medium heat or in a 350°F oven for 2 to 3 minutes.

RECIPE RESCUE: If a grapefruit tastes overly acidic, sprinkle some salt on it to balance the flavor.

SUBSTITUTION: If you can't find ruby red grapefruit, you can substitute regular grapefruit in this salad.

RECIPE RESCUE: If avocados aren't quite ripe enough, place them in a brown paper bag for a few days until ready to use.

STORAGE TIP: Poppy seeds can be stored in an airtight container in the refrigerator for up to 6 months without becoming rancid.

CHICKPEA AND BLACK BEAN SALAD

This recipe has more ingredients than steps to prepare it, and the main two ingredients come in cans, which merely need to be opened! If you want to dress this one up, cut additional red bell peppers into halves and core them. Fill each half with the bean salad, and you have little edible serving bowls—with no dish to clean!

MAKES 4 TO 6 SERVINGS

One 15.5-ounce can chickpeas (garbanzo beans), rinsed and drained

One 15.5-ounce can black beans, rinsed and drained

1 fresh jalapeño pepper, seeded and finely chopped

1 red bell pepper, seeded, cored, and finely chopped, plus extra for
   garnish

½ red onion, finely chopped

½ bunch fresh cilantro, chopped

¼ cup balsamic vinegar

1 tablespoon lemon juice

Salt and freshly ground black pepper

1. In a glass mixing bowl, combine the chickpeas, black beans, jalapeño
   and red bell pepper, onion, cilantro, balsamic vinegar, lemon juice, and
   salt and black pepper to taste. Stir all the ingredients together well.
   Taste and adjust the seasonings.

2. Garnish with extra red bell pepper slices, and serve at room
   temperature or cover and refrigerate until ready to serve.

---

*S*HORT-CUT TIPS

PLAN AHEAD: To speed the chilling of ingredients for salads, store
some of your canned goods, like beans, in the refrigerator before
preparing the salad.

RECIPE RESCUE: Before serving salads that have been refrigerated
or standing, stir them to bring the juices or dressings that have settled
to the bottom to the top. This makes salads taste better and look
fresher.

LEFTOVER PASTA SALAD

Extending the life of a leftover and turning it into another meal is the essence of Short-Cut Cooking, and nothing works better than cooked pasta, which can be served cold. Just add some quickly chopped-up vegetables and some dressing, and in no time you have a wonderful vegetarian entrée salad or a hearty side dish.

MAKES 6 TO 8 SERVINGS

SALAD

½ pound leftover cooked pasta (whatever you have left)

2 tablespoons olive oil, preferably extra-virgin

½ *each* red, yellow, and green bell pepper, cored and seeded, cut into
slivers

1 cup frozen broccoli florets, thawed and drained

4 ounces sun-dried tomato-basil feta cheese (or plain feta), crumbled

½ red onion, cut into thin strips

2 tablespoons capers

¼ cup chopped fresh parsley

¼ cup chopped fresh basil

DRESSING

½ cup chopped ripe tomatoes

3 tablespoons balsamic vinegar

1 tablespoon olive oil

Salt and freshly ground black pepper

> **MINI:**
> You can use fresh broccoli in this recipe. Just steam the florets in a plastic bag with a few holes poked into it in the microwave on high for about 45 seconds. Cool, and add to the salad.

1. To make the salad, in a large bowl, toss the leftover pasta with the olive oil. Add the remaining salad ingredients and toss together well.

2. For the dressing, in a jar, with a tight-fitting lid, combine all the dressing ingredients. Shake well. Adjust the seasonings to taste.

3. Pour the dressing over the pasta salad and toss well. Serve the salad immediately or cover it and refrigerate until ready to serve.

SHORT-CUT TIPS

SHOPPING TIP: Most large supermarkets now carry feta cheeses with added flavors such as sun-dried tomatoes and basil. If you can't find these flavored fetas, just use regular feta cheese and add a bit of chopped sun-dried tomatoes and extra fresh basil to your recipe.

STORAGE TIP: Store cooked pasta in resealable plastic bags in the refrigerator. You can freeze leftover pasta in a plastic freezer bag as well. Let sit at room temperature to thaw.

SOUPS, STEWS, AND SANDWICHES

I can still taste my dad's vegetable soup, made from scratch, which inspired me to try making soups of all kinds. But to save time, I've had to streamline the process. *Country Kitchen* guests supplied me with many ideas for short-cuts and ingredient combinations—Steve Allen's soup was made completely of leftovers, and Pearl Bailey's soup was a hearty combination of zucchini and hamburger.

When we're on boat trips, soups are a must! Our favorites go into a big thermos and we serve them between meals. Chili, a favorite of my husband, is served often. Soup and chili are both easy dishes to store and serve in cramped quarters!

Soups, stews, and sandwiches are always great to serve when you're in a hurry. They cover a wide range of wonderful comfort foods, from "kid-friendly" meals like ham and cheese sandwiches, to dishes inspired by other cultures such as Japanese miso soup and Greek souvlaki. They work as lunch or dinner or for in-between!

Edible Containers: If you don't want to carry home a pot or pan when you bring food to a party, try making containers out of food! Hollow out a large squash or pumpkin for soup, stew, or chili. Hollow out a cabbage for dips, and a large round loaf of bread for nuts and chips. You have to take a bit more care when transporting these to the party, but edible containers mean no clean-up!

SMOOTH AND CREAMY GAZPACHO

To save time, I tend to depend more on prepared items when I make soup these days. Julann Griffin, former wife of Merv and creator of Jeopardy! *showed me the fastest way to create gazpacho soup. If your salad has the right gazpacho ingredients, just put all the leftovers in the blender. If you don't have leftovers at the moment, here's a recipe for a light gazpacho that's a little more traditional. It's versatile, tasty, and good as a starter for grilled foods. Or try it as an entrée accompanied by some great fresh bread.*

MAKES 8 SERVINGS

1½ cups tomato juice (or V-8 juice)

1½ pounds ripe tomatoes, peeled (see Step Saver opposite), seeded, and chopped

1 cup chicken broth (fat-free if available)

1 tablespoon balsamic vinegar

1 tablespoon lemon juice

2 cloves garlic, minced

Salt and freshly ground black pepper

1 to 2 medium cucumbers, peeled, seeded, and chopped

½ medium red onion, minced

2 tablespoons chopped fresh basil

1 tablespoon chopped fresh dill

½ green bell pepper, cored, seeded, and chopped

½ cup sour cream or plain yogurt

MINI:

LEFTOVER QUICK AND EASY CHICKEN BROTH: Add leftover chicken bones, skin, and giblets to 2 quarts of boiling water. Add in a few chunks of celery, onion, carrots, salt, and pepper. Cook for about 30 minutes over medium heat. Let cool. Skim off the fat, strain, and freeze in 1-cup portions for later use.

1. In a large nonreactive bowl, stir together the tomato juice, tomatoes, chicken broth, balsamic vinegar, lemon juice, and garlic. Blend well. Add salt and pepper to taste.

2. Add the cucumbers, red onion, basil, dill, and bell pepper. Blend well.

3. Put 3 cups of the mixture into a blender or food processor and blend until smooth. Add back into the bowl and stir.

4. Stir in the sour cream or yogurt until well mixed. Cover and chill until ready to serve.

SHORT-CUT TIPS

TIME SAVER: To save chopping time, use your food processor for this recipe. Chop the tomatoes, cucumbers, onion, and bell pepper together in the processor bowl. Pour into a mixing bowl and add the remaining ingredients.

STEP SAVER: To peel tomatoes fast, cut an ✕ in the bottom (not the stem end) of each tomato. Plunge them into boiling water and leave for 30 to 60 seconds. Remove from the boiling water and plunge into ice water. The peels will slip right off.

HOUSEHOLD HINT: To clean a blender easily, fill it halfway with hot water, add a few drops of dishwashing liquid, and add a few ice cubes to dislodge any food particles. Run it for a few seconds, then rinse.

MUSHROOM-MISO SOUP

A trip to Japan increased my appreciation for its wonderfully light cuisine. Miso, also called soybean paste or bean paste, is a very important part of the Japanese diet and is eaten in some form almost daily. Most supermarkets here carry at least one kind of miso, usually barley miso, rice miso, or soybean miso. You can also find these at health food or Asian grocery stores. Miso has the consistency of peanut butter and is rich in B vitamins and protein. I've learned to keep it on hand to prepare this soup in a jiffy.

MAKES 4 SERVINGS

½ to ¾ pound wild mushrooms (use a mixture of portobello and
   shiitake), cut into bite-sized pieces

2 tablespoons sesame oil

1 tablespoon chopped fresh ginger

3 tablespoons soy miso

1 cup boiling water

4 cups vegetable broth or chicken broth (fat-free if available)

1 pound firm tofu, cut into small cubes

2 scallions, thinly sliced (use white and green parts)

Crushed red pepper flakes

¼ cup balsamic vinegar, or to taste

1. In a heavy stockpot over medium heat, cook the mushrooms in the sesame oil, stirring constantly, for about 3 minutes. Stir in the ginger.

2. Dissolve the miso in the boiling water and add to the stockpot.

3. Stir in the broth and blend well. Raise the heat to medium-high and bring to a boil, then reduce the heat to low.

4. Add the tofu, scallions, red pepper to taste, and the balsamic vinegar. Stir occasionally until heated through. Serve hot.

Short-Cut Tips

INGREDIENT SAVVY: Tofu, also called soybean curd or bean curd, is made from curdled soy milk, much like cheese is made. It takes on the flavor of its surrounding ingredients when used in cooking, but on its own it's somewhat bland, with a slightly nutty flavor. It has a smooth and creamy texture but is firm enough to slice or cut into cubes. Tofu, like miso, is high in protein and low in fat.

RECIPE RESCUE: Thin miso with a liquid, such as water or broth, before adding it to soups to make sure it blends in smoothly.

RECIPE RESCUE: To rehydrate dried wild mushrooms for use in recipes, soak in warm water, wine, or juice, for 15 minutes. Drain and add to recipes as called for.

STORAGE TIPS: If you use only part of a package of tofu and want to save the rest for another recipe, it must be stored in fresh water. Place the leftovers in a bowl with enough water to cover, in the refrigerator, and change the water daily. It should last about 5 days. You can freeze tofu for up to 3 months, although it will have a chewier texture when thawed.

Miso, usually found in the refrigerator section of the market, is packed in jars, plastic tubs, and plastic bags. After opening, close and refrigerate. Use within 3 months, after which it will lose its flavor.

Chicken and Tomato Tortilla Soup

Tortillas are one of the "basics" to keep in your pantry—I always have a stack on hand. I use them for dips or to wrap foods into sandwiches. Here's how I like to use them in soup.

MAKES 4 TO 6 SERVINGS (OR DOUBLE FOR A CROWD OF BIG EATERS!)

1 tablespoon olive oil

1 medium onion, chopped

2 cloves garlic, chopped (or more to taste)

Pinch of sugar

One 28-ounce can whole tomatoes (with liquid), chopped, or use
     crushed tomatoes

½ cup chopped fresh cilantro (divided)

Three 14.5-ounce cans chicken stock (fat-free if available)

1 tablespoon chili powder, or to taste

1 teaspoon dried basil

1 teaspoon dried thyme

2 bay leaves

2 cups chopped cooked chicken

4 to 5 corn tortillas, cut into thin strips (see Step Saver opposite)

Salt and freshly ground black pepper

½ cup sour cream

2 limes, cut into wedges

1. In a stockpot, heat the olive oil over medium heat. Add the chopped onion and garlic. Cook, stirring, until the onions are translucent, 2 to 3 minutes. Add the sugar and stir well.

2. Add the tomatoes to the pot. Increase the heat to medium high.

3. Stir in ¼ cup of the chopped cilantro and all the chicken stock. Add the chili powder, basil, thyme, and bay leaves.

4. Bring the mixture to a boil and add the chicken chunks. Reduce the heat to low and simmer for about 30 minutes, stirring occasionally.

5. While the soup is simmering, preheat the oven to 425°F. Place the cut tortilla strips on a baking sheet and bake until the strips are crunchy, 6 to 8 minutes. Check often to keep them from overcooking.

6. When the soup is done, add salt and pepper to taste and remove the bay leaves.

7. Serve bowls of hot soup with crispy tortilla strips, sour cream dollops, a sprinkling of the remaining fresh cilantro, and lime wedges to squeeze into the soup.

*S*HORT-CUT TIPS

RECIPE RESCUE: For a too-salty soup or stew, add a thin slice of raw potato, heat for 10 to 15 minutes, then discard the potato slice after cooking. The potato absorbs the salt.

RECIPE RESCUE: To extend the life of leftover flour or corn tortillas, make taco chips out of them. Cut them up, carefully fry them in a skillet in very hot oil, then drain on paper towels to absorb the oil.

TIME SAVER: Buy precooked chicken from the deli or supermarket— either roasted chickens or boneless, skinless chicken breasts. Buy extra, and freeze the chopped chicken for future recipes.

TIME SAVER: Save cutting and oven-crisping time by purchasing salt-free tortilla chips in bags. When a soup recipe calls for crispy tortilla strips, just crumble them in.

STEP SAVER: An easy way to cut tortillas into strips quickly is to use a pizza cutter.

SHOPPING TIP: For less expensive chopped tomatoes, and to save a messy clean-up job on the cutting board, buy whole canned tomatoes. With large scissors, cut the tomatoes right inside the can.

TOMATO-BREAD SOUP

This thick and hearty soup is based on a traditional Tuscan recipe that I enjoyed when I visited friends in Florence, Italy. If you prefer a more liquid soup, add an additional cup of broth.

MAKES 4 SERVINGS

2 tablespoons olive oil

4 cloves garlic, minced

3 tablespoons minced shallots

3 pounds ripe tomatoes, peeled, seeded, and chopped

⅓ cup chopped fresh basil

2 cups chicken broth (fat-free if available)

Salt and freshly ground black pepper

6 slices sourdough French bread, sliced and cut into cubes

Freshly grated Parmesan cheese for garnish

1. In a large pan over medium-high heat, warm the olive oil. Add the garlic and shallots and cook, stirring, until the shallots are softened and translucent, about 3 minutes.

MINI:

EDIBLE SOUP BOWLS: **Choose dense, crusty round loaves of bread and slice off the top of each loaf with a serrated knife. Scoop out half of the inside to form a bowl. Lightly toast, and fill with your favorite soup. It's a simple presentation trick, and there are no bowls to wash after the meal! Place the "bowls" over plates when serving, just to be safe. If served immediately, the bowls should last for about 30 minutes.**

2. Add the tomatoes, basil, and broth to the pan. Stir well. Add salt and pepper to taste. Bring to a boil, then reduce the heat to low.

3. Stir in the bread cubes and cook for about 3 minutes. Remove from the heat. Cover and let stand for about 5 minutes.

4. Serve the soup hot, in individual bowls, garnished with Parmesan cheese.

*S*HORT-CUT TIPS:

TOOL TIP: To make very quick work of jobs like cubing bread, a great kitchen utensil to have on hand is an electric knife.

STORAGE TIP: Freeze fresh herbs in water or broth in ice cube trays for use in soups and stews. When the liquid is frozen, remove the "herb cubes" and store them in plastic bags. Add them to recipes as needed.

SAVORY LENTIL STEW

Because lentils cook very quickly and don't need to be soaked first, they're great to use when you're rushing to make a meal. They're available in great variety and you can use any type you like for this savvy stew—and they're so good for you!

MAKES 4 TO 6 SERVINGS

2 tablespoons olive oil

4 cloves garlic, crushed

1 medium onion, chopped

1 green bell pepper, cored, seeded, and chopped

4 to 5 cups chicken broth or vegetable broth (fat-free if available)

1 cup green or brown lentils, rinsed and drained

1 teaspoon *each* dried oregano, thyme, and basil

Salt and freshly ground black pepper

One 10-ounce package frozen cauliflower florets, thawed

One 28-ounce can whole tomatoes, drained and cut into chunks

3 tablespoons balsamic vinegar

1. In a large stockpot over medium-high heat, warm the olive oil. Add the garlic, onion, and bell pepper. Cook, stirring, until the onion is transparent, 2 to 3 minutes.

2. Pour the broth into the pot and add the lentils. Stir well. Bring to a boil.

3. Add the dried oregano, thyme, and basil, and salt and pepper to taste. Stir well. When the mixture begins to boil, turn the heat down to medium-low and cook, partially covered, until the lentils are soft,

30 to 40 minutes. The mixture should be thickened, but you can add more broth if necessary as it cooks.

4. Stir in the cauliflower and tomato chunks. Cook until they're hot, stirring often. Remove from the heat and stir in the vinegar. Serve hot.

---

*S*HORT-CUT TIPS

MEASUREMENT SAVVY: When measuring dried herbs, fill the measuring spoon lightly and level it off with a knife. Then empty the contents into your hands and crush with your fingers to release the herb oils. Don't crush first and measure second.

RECIPE RESCUE: If you've used too much garlic in a soup or stew recipe, place some parsley flakes in a tea ball and let it simmer in the mixture for about 10 minutes. The parsley soaks up the excess garlic but doesn't remain in the recipe.

STORAGE TIP: When fresh herbs are available in the summer, it's a good time to dry some for later use. Tie bundles of fresh herbs together with kitchen string or ribbon. Hang upside down in a dry, dark place. Cut off and crumble as needed for recipes.

OYSTER AND POTATO STEW

Originally this was a simple oyster stew prepared for me by my friend Phyllis Diller. Phyllis is one of the funniest, smartest people I know and no slouch when it comes to cooking. For a heartier stew, I added ingredients like potatoes to her recipe, and the result is a great combination.

MAKES 6 SERVINGS

3 tablespoons unsalted butter

1 medium yellow onion, chopped

2 ribs celery, chopped

2 carrots, chopped

4 medium Yukon Gold potatoes, cut into bite-sized chunks, unpeeled

Salt and freshly ground black pepper

1 teaspoon paprika

2 bay leaves

1 pint oysters with liquor (see Step Saver opposite)

1 cup light cream

1. Melt the butter in a stockpot over medium-high heat. Add the onion, celery, and carrots and cook, stirring, until the onion is softened, 2 to 3 minutes.

2. Add the potato chunks to the pot and stir well. Pour in enough water just to cover the potatoes. Add salt and pepper to taste. Stir in the paprika and bay leaves.

3. Bring to a low boil. Reduce the heat to medium-low and cook until the potatoes are just fork-tender, about 20 minutes.

4. Add the oysters with their liquor and stir gently. Cook until hot, about 5 minutes.

5. A few minutes before serving, add the cream and heat. Do not boil. Adjust the seasonings. Serve hot.

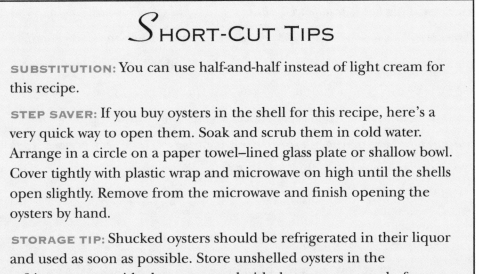

SHORT-CUT TIPS

SUBSTITUTION: You can use half-and-half instead of light cream for this recipe.

STEP SAVER: If you buy oysters in the shell for this recipe, here's a very quick way to open them. Soak and scrub them in cold water. Arrange in a circle on a paper towel–lined glass plate or shallow bowl. Cover tightly with plastic wrap and microwave on high until the shells open slightly. Remove from the microwave and finish opening the oysters by hand.

STORAGE TIP: Shucked oysters should be refrigerated in their liquor and used as soon as possible. Store unshelled oysters in the refrigerator, cup side down, covered with damp paper towels, for no more than 3 days. (Unshelled oysters should be alive when purchased. If live, their shells will be tightly closed. Discard any with open shells.)

FOUR BEAN CHILI WITH BLUE CHEESE–CORNBREAD CROUTONS

There's nothing like a great bowl of chili on a cool fall or cold winter evening. And there are endless types of chili, as my guests on Country Kitchen *demonstrated. Dale Evans made one with no beans, while Glen Campbell created a pinto bean special. I've used pinto beans in this recipe too, plus three other favorite types of beans, to create a wonderful blend of flavor and texture. This chili is rather spicy, which is how I like it. And because so many ingredients can come from cans, it's fast, fast, fast! This is great the next day for leftovers.*

MAKES 8 TO 10 SERVINGS

3 tablespoons olive oil

2 medium yellow onions, chopped

1 red bell pepper, seeded and chopped

4 cloves garlic, crushed

4 canned hot chile peppers, chopped

2 to 4 fresh jalapeño peppers, seeded and diced

Two 28-ounce cans whole tomatoes, chopped (with liquid)

2 tablespoons ground cumin

2 tablespoons chili powder

One 15.5-ounce can Great Northern beans, rinsed and drained

One 15.5-ounce can black beans, rinsed and drained

MINI:

INSTANT BEAN SOUP:
Rinse and drain a can of your favorite beans and add to a saucepan with a can of chicken broth. Warm over medium heat. Add a second can of rinsed, drained, and pureed beans to the pot. Stir well. Season to taste with salt, freshly ground black pepper, garlic powder, Italian seasonings, and chopped fresh parsley.

One 15.5-ounce can kidney beans, rinsed and drained

One 15.5-ounce can pinto beans, rinsed and drained

2 cups fat-free chicken stock

1 cup orange juice

Dash of crushed red pepper flakes

Salt and freshly ground black pepper

Blue Cheese–Cornbread Croutons (recipe follows)

1. Place a large stockpot over medium-high heat and heat the olive oil. Add the onions, red bell pepper, garlic, chile peppers, and jalapeños. Cook, stirring, until the onions begin to turn translucent, about 5 minutes.

2. Add the tomatoes, cumin, chili powder, Great Northern beans, black beans, kidney beans, and pinto beans. Stir together.

3. Pour in the chicken stock and juice. Stir well. Add the red pepper flakes and salt and pepper to taste.

4. Turn the heat to medium-low and cook until the chili is hot throughout, 30 to 45 minutes. Serve with the croutons.

SHORT-CUT TIPS

MEASUREMENT SAVVY: One 15.5-ounce can of beans equals about 1¾ cups, drained.

SANITY SAVER: To remove excess salt from canned beans, always rinse and drain them before use.

HOUSEHOLD HINT: To avoid burning your skin when working with jalapeños, wear plastic or rubber kitchen gloves. Or, use 2 small plastic bags. Cut the pepper away from the core with a sharp knife. Discard both the seeds and core. Chop and add to recipe.

BLUE CHEESE–
CORNBREAD CROUTONS

These croutons are a wonderful addition to chili for added taste and a contrast in texture. They can be combined with many other dishes, and there are endless possibilities for flavoring—depending on what you have handy!

MAKES 8 TO 10 SERVINGS

One 6-ounce package cornbread mix (the "just add water" or the
  "add egg and water" variety)
2 ounces blue cheese, crumbled
1 to 2 tablespoons olive oil
Salt and freshly ground black pepper

1. Preheat the oven to 425°F. Grease a baking pan or cast-iron skillet.

2. Prepare the cornbread mix according to the package directions.

3. Stir in the blue cheese. Take care not to overmix.

4. Pour the mixture into the prepared baking pan or skillet. Bake in the oven until golden brown, about 15 to 25 minutes, depending on the package directions.

5. Remove from the oven and cool on a rack. When cool, cut the cornbread into oversize cubes of about 1½ to 2 inches.

6. Drizzle the cornbread cubes with olive oil and place on a baking sheet. Toast in the 425°F oven until golden brown and crispy, about 6 to 8 minutes.

7. Season the croutons with salt and freshly ground black pepper to taste. When cool, store in a resealable plastic bag in the refrigerator until ready to use.

SHORT-CUT TIPS

HERE ARE A FEW OTHER INTERESTING CROUTON COMBINATIONS.

M I N I :

SOURDOUGH AND PESTO CROUTONS: **Cut good-quality crusty sourdough bread into cubes. Place 1 to 2 tablespoons of premade pesto sauce in a skillet and heat over medium-high. Add bread cubes and cook until the bread is coated with pesto and crunchy.**

M I N I :

PUMPERNICKEL AND GOAT CHEESE CROUTONS: **Cut good-quality pumpernickel bread into thick slices. Spread the slices with a thin coat of softened goat cheese. Cut into cubes and bake until crispy, about 5 to 6 minutes.**

FRESH VEGETABLE AND CRUSTY BREAD SANDWICHES

This sandwich can be made with any of your favorite fresh vegetables and bread. It's my version of the pain bagna, *famous in the south of France where I first tried and fell in love with it! French bread is almost like dessert to me—the crust is out of this world. This is a great to-go meal, and can easily be made a day ahead.*

MAKES 6 SERVINGS (OR MULTIPLY FOR AS MANY AS YOU DESIRE)

1 loaf of good-quality crusty French bread cut into 6 equal pieces

4 to 6 whole cloves garlic, crushed

Olive oil, preferably extra-virgin

Fresh basil leaves, torn into pieces

3 to 4 ripe tomatoes (in the winter months use halved cherry
    tomatoes, they're usually more flavorful), sliced

1 medium red bell pepper, cored, seeded, and cut into silvers

One 8-ounce can artichokes, well drained and quartered

1 medium red onion, thinly sliced into rounds

Balsamic vinegar

Salt and freshly ground black pepper

Options: sliced Swiss, fresh mozzarella, or provolone cheese

1. Cut each piece of the French bread in half lengthwise. Rub the crushed garlic into the cut sides of the bread. Drizzle the olive oil over the cut sides of the bread. Let the bread absorb the oil for a few minutes.

2. Layer each bottom half of bread with some of the basil leaves, sliced tomatoes, slivered bell peppers, artichoke quarters, and red onion slices.

3. Drizzle some of the balsamic vinegar and more olive oil over the vegetables. Add salt and black pepper to taste.

4. Cover the vegetables with the top half of the crusty bread. Wrap each sandwich tightly in plastic wrap. Place the sandwiches in a shallow baking dish or bowl. Place a sheet pan or cookie sheet over the top of the sandwiches and weigh them down with a heavy can (or cans) for about half an hour. This helps the flavors meld into a wonderful sandwich!

5. Unwrap and serve the sandwiches. They make a great "lunch to go."

SHORT-CUT TIPS

SUBSTITUTION: A good substitute for a long loaf of French bread are individual crusty sandwich rolls from the supermarket or bakery. Since you only have to cut lengthwise, you also save time!

TIME SAVER: If you're in a real rush, use prechopped garlic in jars from the supermarket. Always keep some on hand for emergencies. Another option is to use prepackaged pesto.

TIME SAVER: Use packaged precut vegetables such as mushrooms, carrot sticks, or salad mixes in a bag.

PLAN AHEAD: Fresh basil may be hard to find in some areas when it's out of season. So, when you do find it, finely chop up a batch and mix it well with enough olive oil to cover. Store it in a plastic bag in the freezer, and break off pieces as needed. For this recipe, let some thaw, and spread it on the bread, omitting some of the olive oil "drizzle."

HOUSEHOLD HINT: To clean a thermos, fill it with hot water and pour in some salt or baking soda. Let it stand for 5 to 10 minutes, then shake and rinse.

HAM AND SWISS CHEESE TORTILLA ROLL-UP SANDWICHES

Here's another use for one of my favorite "breads"—tortillas! This is a very easy way to update the brown bag lunch, and the kids will love it.

MAKES 4 SERVINGS

4 large (8-inch) flour tortillas

⅓ cup mayonnaise and ¼ cup Dijon mustard mixed together

Leaf lettuce

½ red onion, very thinly sliced

2 ripe tomatoes, thinly sliced

4 to 6 slices of your favorite ham

4 to 6 slices of Swiss cheese

Salt and freshly ground black pepper

1. While you're slicing vegetables, place the tortillas, wrapped in foil, in a 350°F oven, about 5 to 8 minutes. When the tortillas are warm, remove them from the oven.

MINI:

Here are two fun roll-up sandwiches for kids.

PEANUT BUTTER, JELLY, AND BANANA ROLL-UP: **Spread a 6- to 8-inch flour tortilla with peanut butter and jelly. Place a whole banana in the center and wrap the tortilla tightly around the banana. Cut it in half. The kids can eat it with one hand. Or wrap the halves in plastic wrap for packing in lunchboxes.**

HOT DOG AND MUSTARD ROLL-UP: **Smear a 6- to 8-inch flour tortilla lightly with mustard. Place one cooked hot dog in the center and roll it around the hot dog. Cut it in half and serve. Or wrap the halves in plastic wrap for a lunchbox treat.**

2. On each tortilla spread some of the mayonnaise-mustard mixture.

3. Place lettuce leaves over each tortilla. Scatter some of the onion and tomato slices over each.

4. Place slices of the ham and slices of the Swiss cheese on each. Add salt and pepper to taste.

5. Roll up each tortilla gently but firmly. Wrap them in foil and chill for at least 20 minutes. Cut each rolled-up sandwich in half, cover with plastic wrap, and pack in a lunchbox.

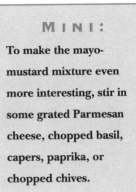

MINI:

To make the mayo-mustard mixture even more interesting, stir in some grated Parmesan cheese, chopped basil, capers, paprika, or chopped chives.

*S*HORT-CUT TIPS

SUBSTITUTION: There are all sorts of presliced cooked hams on the market today. Buy your favorite, smoked or regular, turkey ham, as well as a variety of imported hams. I like precooked sliced turkey too.

TOOL TIP: To make a useful "tortilla warmer," use two terra-cotta saucers (like the kind used under terra-cotta pots in the garden). Use one for the bottom, then top with a second of the same size. Voilà—you have a tortilla warmer!

SOUVLAKI IN PITA BREAD AND TZAZIKI SAUCE

This Greek specialty of marinated lamb chunks, skewered, grilled, and topped with a refreshing sauce of cucumber and yogurt, is a favorite of my favorite guy—my husband! John's parents were from a small town in Greece, and I have lovely memories of our visits there. When we have no time to travel, this easy recipe is a nice substitute.

MAKES 4 TO 6 SERVINGS

2 tablespoons olive oil

2 tablespoons lemon juice

2 tablespoons red wine vinegar

1 tablespoon chopped fresh oregano

2 teaspoons chopped fresh rosemary

Salt and freshly ground black pepper

1½ pounds boneless leg of lamb, cut into 1-inch cubes

4 to 6 pita pocket breads

Tzaziki (recipe opposite) or plain yogurt

1. In a glass or nonreactive bowl, combine the olive oil, lemon juice, vinegar, oregano, rosemary, salt and pepper.

2. Add the lamb cubes to the bowl and marinate in the refrigerator for 30 minutes to 1 hour, or overnight.

3. Heat the grill or broiler. If using a gas or electric grill, set to high.

4. Thread the lamb cubes onto skewers and cook on the grill or in the broiler for about 5 minutes on each side, basting with any extra

marinade while cooking. Remove the meat from the skewers. Serve in pita bread with tzaziki sauce.

SHORT-CUT TIPS

STEP SAVER: If you're in a big hurry, skip the grilling/skewer part of this recipe. Simply cut the lamb into cubes and cook it in a skillet over medium-high heat, stirring, until cooked through, about 10 minutes. Proceed with the recipe as usual.

STORAGE TIP: Since pita bread freezes well, always keep some on hand.

TZAZIKI

This is the traditional accompaniment to souvlaki, although there's no reason it can't be used with other dishes. In fact, I've used it as a dip for chips and vegetable appetizers.

MAKES 4 SERVINGS

2 cucumbers, peeled and diced (seeded if desired—approximately 2 cups)

1 cup plain yogurt

1 tablespoon chopped fresh mint leaves

1 tablespoon olive oil

2 cloves garlic, minced

1 tablespoon fresh lemon juice

Salt and freshly ground black pepper

1. In a nonreactive bowl, mix together all the ingredients. Blend well.

2. Cover the mixture and chill until ready to use. This is great as a sauce with pita sandwiches and other Greek dishes.

M I N I :

This sauce is thicker and richer if made with yogurt cheese instead of just yogurt. To easily make *yogurt cheese:* Line a colander or sieve with cheesecloth and pour in one carton of plain yogurt. Let it drain through the cheesecloth for 1 to 2 hours or overnight in the refrigerator until the excess liquid has drained out.

M I N I :

GREEK YOGURT CHEESE SPREAD: Mix together 1 cup yogurt cheese (see above); $\frac{1}{4}$ cup chopped Greek olives, pitted; a dash *each* of garlic salt and cayenne pepper; and 1 tablespoon chopped fresh parsley. Mix together. Very good on pita toast.

VEGETABLES AND SIDE DISHES

Sometimes it's a challenge to figure out what to serve with a quick entrée, but if you take a fast survey of your pantry, and you've stocked up on your favorite "staples," you'll probably already have everything you need. Any kind of vegetable, potatoes, or rice can be turned into an interesting accent dish if you try combining ingredients you like.

Pair up your favorite vegetables with some leftover rice, sprinkle with fresh herbs, and you've created a presentable side dish. Vegetables, frozen or fresh, can also be steamed, stir-fried, or grilled, and then drizzled with a sauce of sour cream mixed with creamy Italian dressing. Do the same with pasta!

Whether they're baked or mashed, potatoes can be topped with anything from cheese to caviar. Sweet potatoes don't have to wait until Thanksgiving to be served plain or with marshmallows. It's an easy change of pace to have them with canned cranberry sauce any time of year, with or without turkey!

Mix rice with leftover barbecue sauce, or like my friend Marion Ross, the television Mom of *Happy Days*, combine it with lentils, beans, and spices for a Middle Eastern–style treat. Even simpler, try my effortless recipe of rice with nuts and coconut flakes, and you've rounded out a meal that's sure to please everyone!

FRESH BEANS WITH TOASTED NUTS

As country kids, we were raised on fresh beans, which we learned to use in countless kinds of dishes. Here's my version of fresh beans with my favorite toasted nuts. I promise you this stressless side dish is a subtle yet delicious combination.

MAKES 6 SERVINGS

1½ pounds fresh green beans in the pod (green beans, pole beans, lima beans—use one kind or a combination of two or three)

1 tablespoon unsalted butter

1 tablespoon olive oil

¼ cup chopped fresh parsley

½ cup favorite coarsely chopped toasted nuts (cashews, almonds, pecans, page 44)

Salt and freshly ground black pepper

1. Rinse the beans (or peas) in cold water. Trim if necessary.

2. Over medium-high heat, bring a large pot of salted water to a boil. Add the beans and blanch until slightly softened, 3 to 5 minutes. Drain the beans well.

3. In a skillet over medium-high heat, melt the butter and olive oil together. Add the blanched and drained beans. Cook, stirring, until the beans are crispy, soft, and hot, about 3 minutes. Remove the pan from the heat.

4. Sprinkle the beans with the parsley, nuts, and salt and pepper to taste. Toss well. Serve immediately.

SHORT-CUT TIPS

RECIPE RESCUE: Revitalize withered-looking vegetables by standing them in cold salted water for about an hour before cooking.

TOOL TIP: Use your kitchen scissors to quickly trim any stem ends from beans and peas.

SANITY SAVER: I use ¼ cup of chopped parsley in this recipe, but one of the secrets to Short-Cut Cooking is trusting your eyes and taste buds to cut down on preparation time. Just chop fresh parsley to your liking into the pan of cooked beans. If you're a few snips off either way, it won't change the recipe dramatically. Use your eyes, taste, and adjust!

STEAMED VEGETABLES

Zucchini, the Italian version of summer squash, long ago became the basis for a number of my dishes because it's so versatile—delicious cooked or raw. Quick-cooking methods like steaming bring out its taste, and it's particularly delicious grilled. Zucchini combines beautifully with any other vegetables you're likely to have around, as it does in this recipe.

MAKES 4 SERVINGS

4 to 6 medium zucchini, cut into 4-inch-long julienne strips

12 white mushrooms, thinly sliced

1 teaspoon Italian seasoning

¼ cup diced roasted red bell peppers (page 107)

½ cup freshly grated Parmesan cheese

Salt and freshly ground black pepper

1. Bring a pot of salted water to boil over high heat. Place a steamer basket in the pot.

2. Add the zucchini and mushrooms. Steam until they're softened, 3 to 4 minutes

3. Place the steamed vegetables in a bowl and add the Italian seasoning, roasted bell peppers, and Parmesan cheese. Add salt and pepper to taste. Toss well. Serve immediately.

---

*S*HORT-CUT TIPS

TIME SAVER: Alternatively, you can steam the zucchini in a plastic storage bag with a few holes poked in it. Place in the microwave for about 3 minutes. The zucchini has enough moisture to create its own steam.

TIME SAVER: Use an egg slicer to slice mushrooms quickly and evenly.

SHOPPING TIP: You can buy prechopped roasted bell peppers to save time. Remember to rinse and drain them before using.

OVEN-ROASTED ASPARAGUS

I love fresh green asparagus, either served alone as a cold salad or as a warm side dish. They're quick to prepare and delicious just roasted with a few herbs and topped with an accent of cheese.

MAKES 4 SERVINGS

1 tablespoon olive oil

½ teaspoon sesame oil

1 teaspoon minced fresh thyme, or ½ teaspoon dried

½ teaspoon grated lemon zest

1 tablespoon lemon juice

Freshly ground black pepper

2 pounds fresh asparagus, trimmed of any tough stem ends

¼ cup freshly grated Parmesan cheese

1. Preheat the oven to 400°F.

2. In a baking pan or casserole dish, mix together the olive and sesame oils, thyme, lemon zest and juice, and pepper to taste.

3. Add the asparagus and toss to coat with the oil mixture. Loosely cover them with foil and roast until the asparagus is just tender, 15 to 20 minutes, tossing once about midway through the cooking time. Take care not to overcook. Remove the foil for the last 5 minutes of roasting time.

4. Sprinkle with the Parmesan cheese and serve hot.

SHORT-CUT TIPS

SHOPPING TIP: Fresh asparagus is now available almost all year in most large supermarkets. Asparagus should be firm and bright green in color. The tips should be fresh looking and not wilted. Trim any tough stem ends from the stalks of fresh asparagus, but don't toss them out. Freeze them, and with other vegetable trimmings, use them to make vegetable stock.

SQUASH AND PEPPERS ON THE GRILL

When you suddenly find that a few visitors have grown into a crowd needing to be fed, instead of serving hamburgers, you can grill a few vegetables and create some light and tasty veggie burgers. Better still, get your guests involved in the chopping and cooking and you'll have hardly anything to do!

MAKES 4 TO 6 SERVINGS

¼ cup olive oil

4 small zucchini, cut into large chunks

4 small yellow squash, cut into large chunks

1 *each* red, yellow, and green bell pepper, halved, cored, seeded, and cut into very large chunks

1 bunch scallions, trimmed

Salt and freshly ground black pepper

¼ cup balsamic vinegar

1. Preheat the grill or broiler.

2. With a pastry brush, brush the olive oil over the vegetables. Sprinkle with salt and pepper to taste.

3. Place the vegetables either directly on the grill, in a grilling basket, or on a broiler pan under the oven broiler, and cook them until they are well grilled on all sides (3 to 5 minutes per side). The vegetables should be tender. As the vegetables cook, remove them from the heat and transfer to a serving platter or bowl. Drizzle with the balsamic vinegar.

4. Serve the vegetables as a side dish with an entrée or use them to make grilled vegetable sandwiches.

SHORT-CUT TIPS

TOOL TIP: Make a quick herb pastry brush: Cut small stems of fresh herbs such as rosemary, thyme, or chives 3 to 4 inches long. Gather them into a bunch, creating a brushlike cluster, and tie together tightly with string. Attach the cluster to a wooden skewer with additional string, creating a "brush." Use this to dip into oil to brush onto vegetables.

SANITY SAVER: Grilling baskets made especially for grilling small items like cut vegetables prevent the vegetables from falling into the grates of a grill, and save a lot of cleaning-up time. They come in many sizes and are found in most kitchenware stores.

HOUSEHOLD HINT: To extend your counter space easily, place a cutting board over a pulled-out kitchen drawer, making sure the board is wedged securely between the counter edge and the drawer face.

QUICK STIR-FRIED GREENS

I've always enjoyed Chinese cuisine, but a trip to China really got me interested in stir-fried dishes. This recipe is simple to prepare and quick to cook, and complements any entrée. In fact, you can turn it into an entrée just by adding thin strips of chicken, beef, or some shrimp.

MAKES 4 SERVINGS

3 cloves garlic, minced

2 tablespoons sesame oil

2 tablespoons rice wine

2 tablespoons soy or tamari sauce

6 cups fresh spinach leaves, loosely packed

3 cups fresh kale leaves, loosely packed

3 cups shredded bok choy or Napa cabbage

1 tablespoon vegetable oil

¼ cup toasted pine nuts (page 217)

Chopped fresh parsley for garnish

1. In a bowl, whisk together the garlic, sesame oil, rice wine, and soy or tamari sauce.

2. Place the spinach, kale, and bok choy or cabbage in a large bowl and drizzle with the garlic-soy mixture. Toss well.

3. Heat a wok over high heat. When very hot, pour the vegetable oil into the center and swirl it around to coat the sides.

4. Add the greens mixture and toss, stirring quickly, just until they begin to wilt, about 1 minute. Immediately transfer the greens to a warm platter or bowl.

5. Sprinkle the greens with pine nuts and chopped parsley and toss. Serve immediately.

SHORT-CUT TIPS

SUBSTITUTION: Use other greens for this stir-fry, such as broccoli rabe, mustard greens, and turnip greens.

STEP SAVER: Cabbages are very easy to shred, either by hand or in the food processor. The trick to shredding by hand is a very good sharp chef's knife. A food processor fitted with the shredder blade will do as quickly, but you'll have to rinse out the bowl and blade.

SHOPPING TIP: You can now purchase plastic vegetable storage bags with tiny holes in them so you can simply rinse, pat dry, and pop greens directly into the bags. The holes allow the greens to breathe, and this keeps them fresh and crispy.

STORAGE TIP: To keep greens fresh and crisp for 3 to 5 days, when you bring them home from the supermarket or in from the garden, rinse them in cold water and pat them dry gently with paper towels. Wrap them loosely in paper towels and place them in a plastic storage bag in the refrigerator.

YUKON GOLD GARLIC SMASHED POTATOES

A few years ago you could find only one or two kinds of potatoes at most supermarkets, but today we're lucky to have a great variety to choose from. Yukon Gold, whose name I love, is one of my favorites. When cooked, it has the consistency of mashed potatoes before they're even mashed! Here's a recipe for one of my favorite comfort foods. Just remember to heat the milk mixture before adding the potatoes—it keeps them hotter.

MAKES 6 SERVINGS

4 to 6 Yukon Gold potatoes (about 2 pounds), unpeeled and rinsed

Salt

½ cup sour cream

½ cup milk

½ cup chicken broth (fat-free optional)

½ teaspoon garlic powder

1 teaspoon paprika

Salt and freshly ground black pepper

MINI:

POTATO PANCAKES: **In a bowl, mix together 2 cups leftover mashed potatoes, 2 tablespoons chopped onion, 1 egg, 1 tablespoon flour, and salt and black pepper to taste. Blend well. Heat 2 tablespoons of vegetable oil in a nonstick skillet over medium-high heat. Drop the potato mixture by quarter cups into the hot oil and press lightly with a spatula to flatten. Cook until golden brown on both sides. Serve hot. This is a wonderful side dish.**

1. Cut the potatoes into quarters and place them in a large pot with water and a generous pinch of salt. Bring the water to a boil and then reduce the heat to medium-low. Cook until the potatoes are softened enough to mash easily, 15 to 20 minutes. Yukon Golds seem to take less time to cook, so keep an eye on them to make sure they don't fall completely apart.

2. While the potatoes are cooking, in a glass mixing bowl, combine the sour cream, milk, chicken broth, garlic powder, paprika, and salt and pepper to taste. Whisk together well.

3. Cover the bowl loosely with plastic wrap and microwave on high for about 3 minutes.

4. Remove the bowl from the microwave and stir. In a large bowl, add the mixture to the cooked, well-drained potatoes, and mash them with a fork or potato masher. You can use an electric mixer on medium speed if desired.

5. Adjust the seasonings to taste, and serve hot. These are great with meat loaf.

SHORT-CUT TIPS

SUBSTITUTION: If you're out of sour cream, you can make yogurt cheese using plain yogurt. Simply strain through a fine sieve, set over a bowl or sink, until some of the liquid has drained off, 15 to 20 minutes.

PLAN AHEAD: You can freeze leftover mashed potatoes to use later in other recipes, such as the potato pancakes recipe (see Mini opposite). Freeze in plastic freezer bags in portions to suit your family. Thaw by removing the bag from the freezer and placing it in the refrigerator, or follow your microwave oven's instructions for thawing.

ROQUEFORT-STUFFED NEW POTATOES

This recipe was inspired by singer "England Dan" Seals's great potato soup. As usual, I began to experiment with other ingredients and came up with this delicious, quick side dish I might also call "Presto Potatoes"!

MAKES 6 SERVINGS

2 dozen new (waxy) potatoes, unpeeled and rinsed

3 to 5 ounces Roquefort cheese, crumbled

2 tablespoons chopped fresh chives; plus extra for garnish (optional)

½ cup sour cream

Salt and freshly ground black pepper

1. Place the potatoes in a large pot of water and bring to a boil. Reduce the heat to medium-high and boil until the potatoes are cooked but not mushy, about 15 minutes.

2. Use a knife or a melon ball scoop to hollow out the potato until the "skin" of the potato is about ¼ inch thick.

MINI:

This recipe can be easily turned into a "twice-baked potato" dish using large baking potatoes. Bake 2 potatoes until the insides are soft and fluffy, 30 to 45 minutes in a conventional oven. Cut the tops from the baked potatoes while still hot, and put the tops in a mixing bowl. Scoop out the insides of each potato and add to the bowl. Mix in the other ingredients as called for in this recipe, combining them with a fork. Scoop the mashed potatoes back into the "shells." Return them to a hot oven and heat thoroughly.

3. Place the scooped-out potato in a bowl and mash with a fork or potato masher.

4. Add the cheese, chives, sour cream, and salt and pepper to taste. Mix together well with a fork.

5. Fill the potato skins with the potato-cheese mixture. Serve at room temperature, or warmed in a low oven. If desired, garnish with chives.

SHORT-CUT TIPS

SERVING TIP: Top the potatoes with a bit of caviar for a dressier taste, or try cracked black pepper and a bit of sea salt.

SUBSTITUTE: Instead of sour cream, make some tasty *crème fraîche* to use in this recipe for a real treat. Combine 1 cup heavy cream and 2 tablespoons buttermilk in a glass jar. Cover and let stand at room temperature from 8 to 24 hours until very thick. Stir well, cover, and refrigerate. Add a dash of paprika or minced bell pepper for taste.

SWEET POTATO FINGERS

This is an easy side dish to bake in the oven while you do other things, and great to serve at informal gatherings for both kids and adults. If the potatoes are very fresh with thin skins, don't spend time peeling them—they're wonderful as is. You can cook these potato fingers in hot oil as well, just leave them in until they're nice and crispy.

MAKES 4 TO 6 SERVINGS

3 pounds sweet potatoes, unpeeled, cut
   into 3- to 4-inch-long sticks, about
   ½ inch thick

Vegetable oil

Salt and freshly ground black pepper

> **MINI:**
> Turn this recipe into a sweet treat by tossing the potato fingers in a mixture of brown sugar and cinnamon before baking. Bake them until crunchy and serve with applesauce.

1. Preheat the oven to 450°F.

2. Spray a wire cooling rack with nonstick vegetable spray.

3. In a bowl, toss the potato pieces in the oil. Sprinkle with salt and pepper to taste.

4. Place the potatoes flat, not touching, on a wire cooling rack over a baking sheet and bake for 25 to 30 minutes. The potatoes should be soft on the inside and somewhat crispy on the outside.

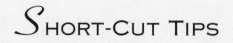

SHORT-CUT TIPS

SUBSTITUTION: Try shaking some seasoning salt instead of salt and pepper on the potato fingers while they're hot. Also try Cajun seasoning salt and garlic salt.

PARMESAN SPAGHETTI SQUASH

This dish is healthy and truly hassle-free! It can be served as a side dish or as an entrée with a salad. If you're really in a big hurry, you can cook it in a microwave. The flavor won't be quite as nutty and rich as when cooked in a conventional oven, but it will still be quite delicious. Just place the squash, cut side down, on a microwave-safe dish, cover it loosely with plastic wrap, and cook it until it's softened, about 5 to 8 minutes.

MAKES 4 TO 6 SERVINGS

One 3- to 4-pound spaghetti squash

2 tablespoons unsalted butter

¼ cup chopped onion

2 cloves garlic, crushed

3 red bell peppers, roasted (see Mini below), cut into slivers

¼ cup basil leaves

Salt and freshly ground black pepper

1 cup freshly grated Parmesan cheese

MAKE-AHEAD MINI:

ROASTED PEPPERS: **If you have a surplus of red bell peppers or find a great deal on them at the market, you can easily make your own roasted peppers when you aren't rushed. Here's how: With the knife point, poke a few holes through the skins of whole red bell peppers and place them on a baking sheet in the oven under the broiler. Broil until the skins begin to turn black. Using tongs, turn the peppers over once while cooking to blacken them on the other side. When almost completely blackened, remove the peppers from the oven and set aside. When the peppers have cooled, the skins slip off easily. Place the roasted peppers, covered with olive oil, in a jar or freeze them in plastic freezer bags.**

1. Preheat the oven to 375°F.

2. Cut the squash in half and scoop out the seeds. Spray a baking pan with nonstick cooking spray and place the squash, cut side down, in the pan. Bake the squash in the oven for about 25 minutes, until it's softened.

3. In a nonstick skillet over medium heat, melt the butter. Add the onion and garlic. Cook, stirring, until they're softened, 3 to 4 minutes.

4. Stir in the roasted peppers and basil. Cook, stirring, for about 3 minutes.

5. Using a fork, pull strands of the spaghetti squash from the cooked squash and add to the skillet. Toss well. Stir until heated through.

6. Add salt and pepper to taste. Remove from the heat.

7. Scatter Parmesan cheese over the mixture and toss well. Adjust the seasonings and serve immediately.

SHORT-CUT TIPS

SANITY SAVER: To safely cut a squash (which is very hard) in half: With a large knife, slice off a piece from one of its sides so it will sit flat on the board. Place the flat side on a damp cloth on a cutting board, to prevent slipping. Insert the tip of a large chef's knife into the squash to begin cutting. This is a good time to use an electric knife if you have one!

ASPARAGUS BASMATI RICE

Basmati rice, with its unique nutty flavor, is great to eat by itself or as an accompaniment to chicken or fish. And it makes your whole house smell wonderful. To flavor it while cooking, add all kinds of ingredients such as cinnamon sticks, bay leaves, dried wild mushrooms, sprigs of fresh herbs, balsamic vinegar, shredded cheeses, and grated orange or lemon zest.

MAKES 4 TO 6 SERVINGS

1 cup uncooked basmati rice

Dash of salt

1 cup chicken broth (fat-free optional)

¾ cup orange juice

2 tablespoons butter

1 pound fresh asparagus, trimmed, cut into 2-inch pieces

Salt and freshly ground black pepper

Strips of orange zest for garnish (optional)

1. In a mesh strainer under cold water, rinse the basmati rice and drain it well.

2. In a saucepan, combine the rice, salt, chicken broth, orange juice, and butter.

3. Over high heat, bring the mixture to a boil. Reduce the heat to medium and cook until the liquid is just even with the top of the rice. Reduce the heat to low, cover, and simmer until the liquid has been absorbed, about 15 minutes. Remove the saucepan from the heat and let it sit for a few minutes.

4. Place the asparagus pieces in a microwavable glass bowl. Cover loosely with plastic wrap and microwave on high for 3 to 4 minutes, until the asparagus is cooked and tender-crisp.

5. Add the steamed asparagus pieces to the rice and toss gently but well. Add salt and pepper to taste. Add the orange zest for garnish, if desired. Serve hot.

---

*S*HORT-CUT TIPS

PLAN AHEAD: Be sure to keep both chicken and beef broth cubes handy in your kitchen. Add 2 broth cubes to hot water to dissolve, then add to the recipes. Chicken broth granules are also available. These can be added directly to soups and sauces.

RECIPE RESCUE: If you want to use fat-free chicken broth and only have a can of regular broth, you can easily skim off the fat. Place the opened can in the refrigerator for about 30 minutes so that the fat will solidify. Then you can easily skim the fat off the top with a spoon.

QUICK SPINACH RISOTTO

This is a wonderful, creamy rice dish that's great alone or as a side dish. Risotto is an Italian rice dish made by stirring hot broth and rice together, usually adding liquid ½ cup at a time until the rice is cooked al dente. Since it's time-consuming, I've created a short-cut method to have this delicious dish without spending lots of time stirring. If you're serving this dish as an entrée, double the ingredients. This recipe is great for a last-minute dinner.

MAKES 4 SERVINGS

1 cup water

½ cup chicken broth

¼ cup apple juice

1 cup Italian arborio rice (available in supermarkets or Italian markets)

2 cups shredded fresh spinach (or 10 ounces frozen, thawed and well drained)

Salt and freshly ground black pepper

¼ cup freshly grated Asiago cheese (or use Parmesan)

2 tablespoons chopped fresh parsley

1. Lightly spray a nonstick skillet with nonstick cooking spray and place the skillet over medium-high heat.

2. Add the water, broth, and apple juice to the skillet. Bring the mixture to a boil.

3. Add the rice and stir well. Reduce the heat to medium. Cook, stirring often, for 10 minutes.

4. Reduce the heat to low and cover the pan. Cook for another 10 minutes, adding a bit more water if necessary halfway through cooking.

5. Remove the cover and stir in the spinach. Add salt and pepper to taste.

6. Remove the pan from the heat and sprinkle the cheese and parsley over the top. Serve immediately.

*S*HORT-CUT TIPS

INGREDIENT SAVVY: Italian arborio rice is high-starch with a shorter and fatter grain than other short-grain rices. The high-starch content is what creates such a creamy texture when making risotto. If you don't have arborio, you can certainly make this dish with regular white short-grain rice, although it will have a different and less creamy character.

SANITY SAVER: To cut down on fat content when cooking, try the many varieties of nonstick cooking sprays on the market. There are the plain vegetable cooking sprays, olive oil sprays, and sprays with flour added to use in baking.

SAVORY COCONUT RICE

I love coconut, and I'm especially delighted to use it in a nondessert role! This is one of those deceptively simple recipes that packs a wallop when it comes to flavor. Coconut and toasted nuts also add a wonderful texture to plain rice and are an appealing way to extend leftovers.

MAKES 4 TO 6 SERVINGS

2 cups water

1 tablespoon butter

Dash of salt

1 cup Jasmine rice (or plain white rice)

¼ cup sweetened or unsweetened flaked
   coconut

½ cup chopped toasted nuts (cashews,
   almonds or hazelnuts, page 44)

> **MINI:**
>
> If you love the taste of coconut, for a much richer flavor, try using 1½ cups water mixed with ¼ cup canned coconut milk for this recipe.

1. In a saucepan over high heat, bring the water, butter, salt, and rice to a boil.

2. Reduce the heat to low, cover the saucepan, and simmer until the rice is cooked and fluffy, about 20 minutes.

3. Remove the saucepan from the heat and add the coconut and nuts. Mix well, fluff the rice with a fork, and serve immediately.

ASPARAGUS BASMATI RICE (PAGE 109)

EGGPLANT AND ROASTED RED BELL PEPPER DIP (PAGE 35) AND
SUN-DRIED TOMATO, BASIL, AND ONION FOCACCIA (PAGE 28)

STEAK AND SHRIMP KEBABS WITH PEANUT SAUCE (PAGE 169)

SPINACH AND GOAT CHEESE PIZZA (PAGE 207)

GRILLED TEQUILA-LIME CHICKEN WITH SAVORY POLENTA AND
FRESH CORN AND BLACK BEAN SALSA (PAGE 144)

HEARTY HOPPIN' JOHN SALAD (PAGE 45) AND
CHICKPEA AND BLACK BEAN SALAD (PAGE 65)

PAPRIKA SCALLOPS WITH KIWI DRIZZLE
WITH MELON SALSA (PAGE 126)

BERRY, BERRY CORNMEAL CAKES (PAGE 238)

FISH AND SEAFOOD

I've always loved fish and seafood, but when I moved from my home in the Midwest to Los Angeles I discovered even more fresh varieties available to enjoy. When my career took me to wonderful locations like Japan, Hong Kong, Singapore, and Australia, my culinary horizons were widened even further. The lobsters are so huge in Australia that American lobsters seem to have been shrunk by comparison!

Now I actually live on a boat in southern California, and get to eat fresh fish that we've caught ourselves, particularly when we travel. But we've been known to take a creative "short-cut" for our seafood dinners by trading magazines with the Mexican fishermen in exchange for their wonderful lobsters and tiger prawns!

Serving fish is a smart way to prepare a fast meal, since it cooks quickly and you can keep it on hand in the freezer. It rarely requires much equipment to prepare, which is important when you're concerned about storage space (as I am living on the boat). Most of my recipes call for fruits and vegetables as accompaniments, because I appreciate the "leanest" preparations. They're not intentionally "dietetic," but you'll find that for the most part, these recipes are healthy and low in fat, yet high in flavor.

PAN-SEARED FISH
WITH CITRUS RELISH

Phyllis Diller was such a great hit on Country Kitchen *the first time that she visited again, the next time with a wonderful fish recipe which inspired me to develop this one. Hers featured orange roughy, which works well with this citrus relish. But you can use your own favorite fish, such as tuna, halibut, or salmon. This fish entrée is simple to prepare and stunning to serve.*

MAKES 4 SERVINGS

1 tablespoon vegetable oil

Fresh lemon or lime juice

Paprika

Salt and freshly ground black pepper

4 fish steaks (about 6 ounces each), such as tuna, halibut, or salmon,
    rinsed and patted dry

Citrus Relish (recipe opposite)

1. Heat the vegetable oil in a nonstick skillet over medium-high heat until very hot.

2. While the skillet is heating, sprinkle the lemon juice, paprika, and salt and pepper to taste over both sides of the fish.

3. Add the fish steaks to the skillet and cook for about 5 minutes each side. The cooked fish should flake easily. Serve immediately or cover loosely and place in a warm oven to keep hot. Spoon the citrus relish over the fish when serving.

SHORT-CUT TIPS

SUBSTITUTION: Other fish that can be used in this recipe are shark, mahimahi, red snapper, or orange roughy.

SANITY SAVER: If you're using frozen fish steaks, add them to the pan while they're still frozen, since they lose much of their natural moisture if thawed completely. Cook a few minutes longer to make sure fish is completely done inside

STORAGE TIP: To keep raw fish fresh and odorless, rinse it with fresh lemon juice and water, then dry thoroughly. Wrap in plastic wrap, then refrigerate on the bottom shelf of the refrigerator, which is the coldest shelf.

CITRUS RELISH

This relish is perfect with fish, but you can certainly use it as a topping or dip for any other foods you enjoy. **MAKES ABOUT 3 CUPS**

¼ cup minced red onion

1 orange, peeled, seeded, and chopped

1 tangerine, peeled, seeded, and chopped

½ ruby red grapefruit, peeled, seeded, and chopped

½ cup chopped fresh pineapple

1 clove garlic, minced

¼ cup minced red bell pepper

2 tablespoons balsamic vinegar

2 teaspoons light or dark brown sugar

Juice of 1 lime

1 fresh habanero chile pepper, minced

1. In a large glass or nonreactive bowl, mix together the onion, orange, tangerine, grapefruit, and pineapple. Toss well.

2. Add the garlic and the bell pepper. Toss well again.

3. In a small bowl, mix together the vinegar, brown sugar, and lime juice. Drizzle this over the orange mixture. Add the habanero pepper to taste. Toss together well. Serve immediately or cover and refrigerate until ready to serve. Can be stored in the refrigerator for about 2 weeks.

S HORT-CUT TIPS

MEASUREMENT SAVVY: One medium onion is equivalent to about ½ cup of chopped onion. A larger onion may yield 1 cup.

STEP SAVER: When removing seeds from citrus, hold the fruit over a bowl to catch the juice. Add this juice to the recipe you're making or save it for later use.

SANITY SAVER: Habanero peppers are one of the hottest fresh peppers on the market, so a little goes a long way. Wear rubber or plastic gloves while working with these, and be sure not to touch your eyes.

PARCHMENT-BAKED FISH AND SHREDDED VEGETABLES

Parchment paper, which is heavy and water- and grease-resistant, is a great item to have on hand since it has so many uses in the kitchen—lining baking pans or wrapping foods to be baked, like the fish in this recipe. Parchment is a great way to keep baked fish moist and it makes for a great presentation. You can find this paper in gourmet and kitchen stores, as well as in most large supermarkets. And if you serve this dish with a package of frozen cooked rice, prepared according to package directions, you'll be able to whip up a last-minute dinner in no time!

MAKES 4 SERVINGS

4 sheets of parchment paper (or aluminum foil), 12 by 12 inches

Olive oil (enough to coat the parchment paper)

4 fish fillets (6 to 8 ounces each), such as salmon, orange roughy, red snapper, rinsed and patted dry

Paprika

Salt and freshly ground black pepper

2 cups shredded vegetables—a mixture of carrots, zucchini, yellow squash, shallots, or any of your favorites

1 tablespoon chopped fresh dill and Italian parsley combined

1. Preheat the oven to 425°F.

2. Fold each square of parchment paper in half to crease it. Spread it out flat on a work surface and rub one side of each sheet with olive oil.

3. Place 1 fish fillet in the middle of each oiled side. Sprinkle the fillets with some of the paprika, salt, and pepper to taste.

4. Place some of the shredded vegetables on top of each piece of fish.

5. Sprinkle the fresh herbs over the top of the vegetables. Sprinkle all over again with more paprika and salt and pepper to taste.

6. Drizzle about 2 teaspoons of olive oil lightly over each.

7. Fold the second half of the parchment over the fish and vegetables. Beginning on one side, fold the edge over. Repeat, folding it a second time to seal the edge well. Repeat for the other sides. Follow the process with the remaining fillets.

8. Place the parchment packets on a baking sheet. Bake in the oven for about 15 minutes, until they are puffed. Serve the fish and vegetables in the paper immediately. Slice a big ✗ in the top of the paper, and peel it back.

SHORT-CUT TIPS

SERVING TIP: There are many ways to wrap foods for a wonderful presentation. Parchment, aluminum foil, brown craft paper, banana leaves, soaked corn husks, grape leaves, cabbage leaves, or lettuce leaves can all be used as inexpensive, handy wrappers.

TIME SAVER: To quick-slice vegetables, use a vegetable peeler! You'll have "ribbonlike" thin slices that will cook more quickly.

HOUSEHOLD HINT: To prevent your hands from smelling fishy, rinse them with cold water and rub with half a lemon after handling fish.

TOASTED SESAME AND GINGER–CRUSTED TUNA

Living on the West Coast on the ocean means I get to cook with really fresh seafood. In this recipe, I've combined my love of Japanese cuisine and fresh fish to create a very easy and delicious dish. The "kick" comes from wasabi, the Japanese horseradish with a wonderfully sharp and pungent taste. You can buy it most easily in the dried or paste form. Just remember that a little of it goes a long way!

MAKES 4 SERVINGS

2 teaspoons wasabi powder

1½ teaspoons water

½ cup (1 stick) unsalted butter, softened

4 whole scallions, minced

2 to 3 cloves garlic, minced

1 tablespoon Dijon-style mustard

1 teaspoon sugar

2 egg yolks

1½ tablespoons minced fresh ginger

½ cup plus 2 tablespoons toasted sesame seeds (page 44)

1 cup dried bread crumbs, plain or seasoned

4 tuna steaks (about 6 to 7 ounces each), or try halibut

½ cup tamari sauce

½ cup orange juice

3 tablespoons olive oil

1. In a glass mixing bowl, combine the wasabi powder and the water. Mix until a paste forms.

2. Add the softened butter, scallions, garlic, mustard, sugar, egg yolks, ginger, ½ cup of sesame seeds, and the bread crumbs. Mix together well.

3. Rinse the tuna steaks and pat with paper towels until the steaks are very dry.

4. Pat some of the wasabi-crumb mixture onto each steak, covering each well.

5. In a small bowl, combine the tamari, orange juice, and remaining 2 tablespoons of sesame seeds.

6. In a skillet over medium-high heat, heat the olive oil. When the oil is hot, add the tuna to the skillet. Reduce the heat to medium-low and cook the steaks for about 5 minutes on each side. A crust should begin to form and turn brown on each piece of fish. The tuna should be moist but cooked throughout.

7. Serve the tuna hot with a drizzle of the tamari sauce mixture.

SHORT-CUT TIPS

STORAGE TIP: You can store fresh unpeeled gingerroot, tightly wrapped, in the refrigerator for up to 2 weeks. You can store frozen gingerroot for up to 2 months. Store whole roots, remove, and slice off what you need, then return to the freezer.

FRESH TUNA TACOS

I loved the taco chip salad that country singer Tanya Tucker once made for me. It reflected her childhood in the Southwest and featured classic ingredients like avocados, black olives, and nacho cheese. I call this recipe the "West Coast" version, because I fill my tortillas with tuna, tamari, and cilantro. These tacos are light and delicious, pretty to serve, and a great example of the versatility of tortillas.

MAKES 6 SERVINGS

8 to 10 ounces fresh tuna, rinsed and patted dry

2 tablespoons tamari sauce (or soy sauce)

1 cup good-quality chunky salsa, well drained

¼ cup good-quality mayonnaise (or plain yogurt)

6 large corn tortillas

¼ small head green cabbage, finely shredded

¼ cup chopped fresh cilantro

3 whole limes, cut into quarters

1. Place the fresh tuna steaks in a glass baking dish and drizzle with the tamari sauce. Let stand for about 15 minutes. Meanwhile, preheat the oven to broil.

2. When the broiler is ready, place the baking dish with the tuna under the broiler and broil, turning it once, until the tuna is cooked, 4 to 5 minutes on each side. The tuna should be flaky. Remove the tuna from under the broiler and let cool for 5 minutes.

3. In a small bowl, mix together the chunky salsa and the mayonnaise. Stir well.

4. Cut the tuna into chunks.

5. Lay the tortillas out on a flat surface and place some of the chunks of tuna in the center of each. (If preferred, you can wrap the stacked tortillas in foil and heat then in a hot oven for 10 minutes.)

6. In another bowl, mix together the cabbage and cilantro. Scatter some of the cabbage mixture over the tuna.

7. Spoon some of the salsa mixture over the center of each tortilla.

8. Roll the tortillas over the filling. Serve lime quarters with them to squeeze over the tacos.

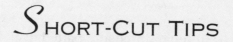

SHORT-CUT TIPS

SUBSTITUTION: You can use regular corn tortillas for this recipe or try the "blue" corn tortillas on the market today.

TIME SAVER: Cook the tuna in the microwave if you're in a really big hurry. After you let the tuna and tamari sauce marinate for 15 minutes, cover it loosely with plastic wrap and microwave on high until it's cooked through, about 3 minutes. Proceed with the recipe as usual.

TIME SAVER: To quickly shred cabbage, use a food processor.

HOUSEHOLD HINT: To disguise fishy odor in your house, use spices to make a reusable potpourri. In a small saucepan, combine some spices like the one you might use during the holidays, such as cinnamon sticks, bay leaves, lemon or orange peel, allspice, or any of your favorites, with some water. Cook over low heat for 2 to 3 minutes, until the aroma permeates the air. If you prepare fish often, you may wish to dedicate a little saucepan specifically for this use, and set the mixture aside in the refrigerator. It can be reused many times.

SMOKED SALMON CAKES

My favorite school lunches were salmon cakes dipped in cornmeal and lightly fried.
My updated version of the classic salmon croquette is light by comparison and makes
a very fine entrée. Use the dry smoked salmon from the deli section of your
supermarket, but not lox, which is too moist and salty and won't crumble properly.
Smoked salmon has a less strong, but nice woody flavor. This recipe works well using
smoked trout or catfish. If you have some time to plan ahead, make the salmon cake
mixture for this recipe earlier in the day, and chill it until you're ready to cook it.

MAKES 4 SERVINGS

½ pound smoked salmon, crumbled (do not use lox, remove and
  discard any skin or bones)

1 large egg, lightly beaten

1 generous tablespoon chopped fresh dill, or 1 teaspoon dried

½ cup mayonnaise (regular or low-fat)

1 teaspoon prepared mustard

Dash of cayenne pepper

Salt and freshly ground black pepper

1 cup saltine cracker crumbs

2 teaspoons fresh lemon juice

2 tablespoons butter

2 tablespoons olive oil

Caper-Tartar Sauce (recipe on page 125)

1. Place the crumbled smoked salmon in a glass mixing bowl.

2. In another bowl, combine the egg, dill, mayonnaise, mustard, cayenne, and salt and pepper to taste. Whisk together well.

3. Scrape the egg mixture into the bowl with the salmon.

4. Add the cracker crumbs and lemon juice. Blend the ingredients well. The mixture will be somewhat dry, but will stick together when it's formed into cakes.

5. In a skillet over medium heat, melt the butter and olive oil together.

6. While the butter mixture is heating, form the salmon mixture into 8 cakes. Cook the salmon cakes in the hot oil until they're golden on both sides, about 12 minutes total. Turn them gently using a spatula. Serve them with the Caper-Tartar Sauce.

*S*HORT-CUT TIPS

TIME SAVER: Make extra salmon cakes and freeze them individually in plastic bags for later use.

SANITY SAVER: The egg mixture used in this recipe won't stick to your hands if you dip them in water before forming the cakes.

MESS SAVER: To crush the crackers, place in a sealable plastic bag, press out most of the air, and seal the top. Roll it with a rolling pin until well crushed.

CAPER-TARTAR SAUCE

Here's a great little accompaniment for any number of fish recipes. Just whip it up with some of the prepared ingredients you should keep in your pantry. Use it as a dip, too!

MAKES ABOUT ¾ CUP

½ cup mayonnaise (regular or low-fat)

1 tablespoon prepared mustard

1 tablespoon fresh lemon juice

Dash of Worcestershire sauce

1 tablespoon pickle relish, well drained

2 tablespoons capers, well drained

1 tablespoon minced scallion whites

Freshly ground black pepper

Dash of hot pepper sauce

1. In a glass bowl, mix together the mayonnaise, mustard, lemon juice, Worcestershire sauce, relish, capers, and scallions.

2. Add the pepper and hot pepper sauce to taste. Blend gently. Cover and chill until ready to serve.

*S*HORT-CUT TIPS

SUBSTITUTION: If you don't have any pickle relish, simply mince some dill pickles and proceed with the recipe as directed.

STEP SAVER: If you need just a little juice from a lemon, pierce it with a fork and squeeze out the desired amount. Then return it to the refrigerator.

PAPRIKA SCALLOPS WITH KIWI DRIZZLE AND MELON SALSA

When company's coming and you're in a hurry, scallops are perfect to serve because they cook so quickly—only about 2 to 3 minutes per side. Be careful not to overcook them, because, like all other shellfish, they'll toughen. This dish features the large sea scallops, which are more widely available and less expensive than the smaller bay scallops. The kiwi drizzle makes a light, refreshing addition to the subtle flavor of the scallops. To remove the kiwi fruit from its peel easily, simply cut it in half and scoop out the fruit with a spoon!

MAKES 4 SERVINGS

KIWI DRIZZLE

4 kiwi fruit, peeled

2 teaspoons sugar

1 tablespoon white wine or white grape juice

SCALLOPS

2 tablespoons paprika

½ cup all-purpose flour

Salt and freshly ground black pepper

2 pounds large sea scallops, rinsed and patted dry

Vegetable oil

Melon Salsa (recipe on page 128)

1. To make the drizzle, place the kiwi in a food processor bowl fitted with the metal blade, and process them until almost smooth. Add the sugar

and white wine. Process until smooth. Pour the mixture into a bowl and chill it until you're ready to serve the scallops.

2. To prepare the scallops, in a mixing bowl, combine the paprika, flour, and the salt and pepper to taste. Add the scallops and toss well to coat them.

3. Heat the oil in a nonstick skillet over medium-high heat. When the oil is very hot, add the scallops. Sear them for about 2 minutes on one side until golden and crispy. Turn the scallops over and cook on the second side until the scallops are cooked throughout, 2 to 3 minutes more. Using a spatula, remove the scallops to a heated platter. Cover loosely and put in a warm oven until ready to serve. Do not let the scallops dry out, and do not overcook.

4. To serve, drizzle some of the kiwi on each dinner plate in a decorative pattern.

5. Arrange the scallops on top of the sauce. Serve hot with the Melon Salsa.

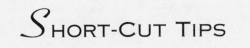

SHORT-CUT TIPS

SHOPPING TIP: Buy scallops that are an ivory color, not snow white. If they're too white, they may have been soaked in water to increase their weight.

MELON SALSA

This fruit salsa is a cool-hot-sweet combination that makes a great sauce for shellfish like scallops. Jalapeños add a little "bite," the melons cool it off, and the honey sweetens it. You can use it as you would any salsa, as a garnish or a dip, for meals or appetizers. **MAKES 4 SERVINGS**

1 cup chopped ripe cantaloupe

½ cup chopped ripe honeydew melon

½ cup chopped ripe plums

½ cup chopped fresh papaya

¼ cup minced red bell pepper

1 to 2 jalapeño peppers, cored, seeded, and minced

¼ cup lime juice

2 teaspoons honey

Salt

2 tablespoons chopped fresh parsley

2 tablespoons chopped fresh cilantro

1. In a glass or nonreactive bowl, combine the fruit and peppers.
2. In a small bowl, whisk together the lime juice, honey, and salt to taste.
3. Drizzle the juice mixture over the fruit. Scatter the parsley and cilantro over all. Toss well. Cover and chill until ready to serve.

SHORT-CUT TIPS

SERVING TIP: Use the shell of the scooped-out papaya as a serving container for any extra salsa.

SUBSTITUTION: Instead of plums, try to use fresh Bing (or any sweet) cherries, if they're in season. The flavor is wonderful and the few minutes it takes to pit them is worth it.

SUBSTITUTION: Maple syrup can be substituted for honey or sugar in a recipe, if you just cut back on the liquids used. Like honey and molasses, the darker the maple syrup, the stronger the flavor.

MEASUREMENT SAVVY: One pound of plums equals six to eight 2-inch whole plums or 3 cups of sliced or chopped plums.

RECIPE RESCUE: If your honey crystallizes, place the jar in a pot of steaming hot water. The crystals will melt and the honey will return to a usable state. You can also use the microwave—just remove the lid of the honey jar, and heat the honey for 20 seconds at a time, stirring after each heating.

TOOL TIP: If you love fresh cherries, an inexpensive pitter is a great investment. If you don't own a cherry pitter, substitute the tip of a vegetable peeler or the point of a knife.

SHOPPING TIP: When in a hurry, buy the peeled and sliced papaya in jars found in most supermarket produce sections. Just drain, chop, and add to the recipe as usual. Prechopped cantaloupe and honeydew melon can often be found at supermarket salad bars.

GOURMET-ON-THE-RUN
EASY CLAM SAUCE

If you keep some basic items on hand in your pantry, with just a few fresh ingredients you'll always be ready to whip up what I call "gourmet-on-the-run" meals. These aren't just fast, they're the special flavors and ingredients that turn an ordinary meal into a more sophisticated experience—the essential additions! For this recipe, try some of the wonderful fresh pastas now available at most large supermarkets, such as red pepper fettuccine, sun-dried tomato linguine, or spinach tortellini.

MAKES 4 SERVINGS

1 tablespoon olive oil

2 cloves garlic

Two 6.5-ounce cans chopped or minced clams, partially drained

One 14.5-ounce can Italian-style tomatoes with juice

1 teaspoon dried Italian seasonings

Salt and freshly ground black pepper

2 tablespoons chopped fresh basil

1 pound favorite pasta, cooked until al dente

Freshly grated Parmesan cheese for garnish

1. In a nonstick skillet over medium-high heat, heat the olive oil. Add the garlic and cook, stirring, until it is softened, about 1 minute.

2. Stir in the clams, tomatoes, Italian seasonings, and salt and pepper to taste. Cook over medium-low heat, stirring occasionally, for 10 to 12 minutes.

3. Remove the skillet from the heat and scatter the basil over all. Stir to combine. Adjust the seasonings to taste and toss with your favorite pasta. Garnish with Parmesan cheese.

SHORT-CUT TIPS

SUBSTITUTION: Make this a "tuna pasta" by using a can of drained tuna instead of the clams. The rest of the recipe remains the same.

SUBSTITUTION: Make a vegetarian gourmet pasta sauce by using artichoke hearts, roasted bell peppers, and capers instead of clams or tuna.

MARINARA MUSSELS WITH LINGUINE

Fresh, live mussels are one of best deals in a supermarket. They're inexpensive, easy to prepare, and low in calories! When you bring them home, rinse the mussels and discard any that have already opened. Right before cooking, use a knife to remove any "beard," and rinse them again in a colander and drain. Clams or shrimp are also great with this speedy seafood sauce.

MAKES 4 TO 6 SERVINGS

2 tablespoons olive oil

2 teaspoons chopped garlic

One 28-ounce can Italian-style tomatoes with liquid, chopped

¼ cup chopped fresh basil

¼ cup chopped fresh parsley

½ teaspoon crushed red pepper flakes

½ cup white wine (optional, or use nonalcoholic wine or clam juice)

Salt and freshly ground black pepper

2 pounds fresh, live mussels, beards removed, rinsed and scrubbed

1 pound linguine, cooked al dente

Freshly grated Romano cheese for garnish

1. In a Dutch oven or other large, heavy saucepan over medium-high heat, heat the olive oil.

2. Add the chopped garlic and cook until it is softened, about 1 minute.

3. Stir in the tomatoes, basil, parsley, red pepper flakes, white wine, and salt and pepper to taste. Bring the mixture to a boil. Reduce the heat to low and simmer for 5 minutes.

4. Add the mussels and cover the pan. Cook until the mussels have opened, 6 to 7 minutes. (Remove and discard any mussels that have not opened.)

5. To serve, place the pasta in a large serving bowl and add the sauce. Toss well. Garnish the individual servings with Romano cheese.

SHORT-CUT TIPS

SANITY SAVER: To chop parsley quickly, don't worry about tearing the leaves off their stems individually. Simply cut the stems of the entire bunch as close as possible to the leaves. The stems are tender, and won't affect the recipe. Make sure the parsley is dry to make chopping easy.

POULTRY

One of the most popular categories of recipes prepared on *Country Kitchen* was poultry—by celebrities as diverse as Dick Van Patten and Terry Bradshaw to Garth Brooks and Dr. Ruth. Like the rest of us, they appreciated its affordability, as well as its versatility in combining with so many other foods and inexpensive ingredients. Actress Michele Lee told me that a favorite dish was her aunt's baked chicken fillets, which she discovered was made with an envelope of onion soup mix, a bottle of French dressing, and a jar of jam!

Most people I know love chicken and turkey, which can be purchased in most supermarkets around the country precut, precooked, elaborately prepared, and ready to heat up. It can be kept frozen for last-minute meals and, as you can see from the wide variety of recipes here, combined with many ingredients to re-create almost any international cuisine at home.

Always be prepared for a last-minute meal by keeping frozen chicken breasts on hand. Boneless, skinless chicken breasts can be purchased in large, affordable packages, holding eight to twelve breasts. When you get the package home, divide the breasts, two or four per smaller plastic freezer bag, for your favorite recipes. Since they're usually 6 to 8 ounces each in weight, they're easily thawed at the end of a hard day. Use your microwave to defrost more quickly. And no matter how you prepare your chicken, be sure to cook it thoroughly!

CHICKEN PICCATA WITH PINE NUTS AND CAPERS

This dish is a perfect example of combining your pantry staples, using what's on hand, and adapting and substituting. Piccata is traditionally made with veal—and it's delicious. But most people have chicken in the freezer or the refrigerator, since it's generally less expensive. You can also substitute turkey or pork, and for vegetarians, this dish can be made with portobello mushrooms or thin slices of eggplant instead of the chicken.

MAKES 4 SERVINGS

½ cup milk

2 large eggs, slightly beaten

½ cup all-purpose flour

Salt and freshly ground black pepper

Four boneless, skinless chicken breasts (6 ounces each), pounded
    into thin pieces

¼ cup (½ stick) unsalted butter

¼ cup vegetable oil

⅓ cup lemon juice

⅓ cup white wine (or apple juice, white grape juice, or chicken broth)

2 cloves garlic, chopped

2 tablespoons capers, rinsed and drained

¼ cup minced fresh parsley

½ pound spaghetti, cooked al dente

¼ cup toasted pine nuts (page 44)

1. In a small bowl, mix together the milk and eggs.

2. Place the flour in another dish; season with salt and pepper to taste.

3. Dip the chicken pieces into the milk mixture and then into the flour mixture. Coat each piece well. Shake off the excess.

4. In a large, shallow skillet over medium-high heat, heat 2 tablespoons of the butter and all the vegetable oil.

5. Add the coated chicken pieces to the hot skillet and cook until the chicken is no longer pink on the inside, about 4 minutes on each side.

6. Remove the chicken from the pan and drain it on paper towels. Set it aside and keep warm.

7. Reduce the heat to medium-low and add the remaining 2 tablespoons of butter to the pan drippings. Stir in the lemon juice, wine, and garlic. Stir well. Cook for 2 to 3 minutes.

8. Add the capers and parsley. Cook, stirring, for about 1 minute.

9. To serve, place a serving of pasta on each plate and top with a breast. Spoon sauce over each and sprinkle with pine nuts. Serve immediately.

---

*S*HORT-CUT TIPS

RECIPE RESCUE: To revive tender fresh herbs, wash them quickly under cold running water and then shake gently to remove excess water. Pat dry gently with paper towels.

TOOL TIP: If you don't have a meat mallet, you can easily use a (very clean) hammer to pound the chicken for this recipe.

MESS SAVER: Use kitchen scissors to trim any excess fat from the chicken.

MESS SAVER: Place the chicken breasts inside a plastic freezer bag before pounding them and you'll have no cutting board to clean up!

INGREDIENT SAVVY: Capers usually come in jars packed in a vinegar brine or salted. Stored in their brine, they'll last for months. To make sure they're completely covered with brine, add some vinegar to the liquid. Rinse them in a small wire-mesh sieve before using to remove some of the salt and vinegar taste.

CRISPY OVEN-BAKED CHICKEN

This is truly one of my favorites, and since there's no frying or oil in this recipe, it's a great way to have lower-fat "fried chicken." Substitutes for crunchy coatings can range from crushed cereal to corn chips or tortilla chips. You can even use crushed nuts. It's another recipe I've developed by using what's on hand in the pantry!

MAKES 4 SERVINGS

One 3½-pound chicken, skin removed, cut into pieces, rinsed and
    patted dry

¼ cup plain yogurt

1 tablespoon Dijon-style mustard

Dash of hot pepper sauce

1 cup crushed saltine crackers

1 cup unflavored dry bread crumbs

¼ cup freshly grated Parmesan cheese

2 teaspoons paprika

2 tablespoons chopped fresh parsley

Dash of cayenne pepper

Salt and freshly ground black pepper

1. Preheat the oven to 375°F. Spray a large baking dish with nonstick cooking spray.

2. Place the chicken pieces in a microwave-safe dish and cover loosely with plastic wrap. Microwave on high until the chicken pieces are halfway cooked, 6 to 8 minutes. You may have to do this in batches.

3. In a shallow bowl, mix together the yogurt, mustard, and hot pepper sauce. Add the chicken pieces and toss well.

4. In a large plastic or paper bag, combine the crackers, bread crumbs, cheese, paprika, parsley, cayenne, and salt and black pepper to taste. Shake together well.

5. Drop the chicken pieces, one at a time, into the bag and shake well, coating each piece of chicken with the mixture. Repeat with all of the chicken pieces.

6. Remove the chicken pieces from the bag and place them in the prepared baking dish. Bake in the oven for 30 to 45 minutes, until the pieces are golden brown and the chicken juices run clear. Serve hot from the oven, or at room temperature for picnics.

SHORT-CUT TIPS

TIME SAVER: Buy boxes of cracker crumbs already crushed in the supermarket.

SANITY SAVER: If you need a warm serving bowl, you can zap it in the microwave (make sure the bowl is microwave safe) or soak it in hot water for a few minutes.

MESS SAVER: To crush the crackers, place in a sealable plastic bag, press out most of the air, and seal the top. Roll it with a rolling pin until the crackers are well crushed.

CHICKEN AND PASTA DIABLO

This recipe is a good example of how chicken lends itself to a variety of seasonings and cooking techniques. The sweet ingredients offset the heat of the peppers, and since everything goes into one skillet, there's less to clean. Another good short-cut is to use precooked chicken so you can add it as quickly as the rest of the ingredients. You'll have your hurried hot and spicy meal on the table in no time!

MAKES 4 SERVINGS

1 pound fettuccine

2 tablespoons olive oil

1 small yellow onion, chopped

1 yellow or red bell pepper, cored, seeded, and chopped

2 tablespoons minced habanero peppers

2 firm, ripe bananas, sliced

⅓ cup pineapple juice

⅓ cup orange juice

¼ cup lime juice

Four cooked skinless, boneless chicken breasts (6 ounces each), cut
       into ¼-inch strips

Salt and freshly ground black pepper

¼ cup freshly grated Parmesan cheese

1. Cook the fettuccine according to the package directions until al dente. Meanwhile, continue with the recipe.

2. In a large saucepan over medium heat, heat the oil. Add the onion, bell pepper, and habanero peppers. Cook, stirring, until softened and the onion is translucent, about 3 minutes.

3. Stir in the bananas, pineapple, orange, and lime juices. Cook until the bananas are softened, about 3 minutes.

4. Add the chicken strips. Heat thoroughly. Add salt and pepper to taste.

5. When the fettuccine is done, drain well. Place the fettuccine in a heated serving bowl. Add the sauce and toss together well until the pasta is coated.

6. Sprinkle with Parmesan and serve hot.

---

*S*HORT-CUT TIPS

PLAN AHEAD: If your bananas are too green, quicken the ripening process by placing them in a brown paper bag with a ripe apple or pear. Gases from the other fruit cause the banana to ripen more quickly.

RECIPE RESCUE: If you want to reduce the strength of hot chiles, scrape out the seeds and membranes and discard.

SANITY SAVER: Habanero peppers are one of the hottest fresh peppers on the market, so a little goes a long way. Wear rubber or plastic gloves while working with these, and be sure not to touch your eyes.

CHICKEN TAMALE PIE

This dish is something like a chili casserole, topped with cornbread, much loved by my daughter Lizzie and her husband, Doug. It's versatile, since you can adjust the seasonings from mild to really spicy, and you can serve it right from the oven in its own casserole dish. If you use small baking dishes instead, you'll have individual servings, and you can call each a "Mexican Potpie"!

MAKES 4 TO 6 SERVINGS

2 tablespoons vegetable oil

1 large onion, chopped

4 cloves garlic, minced

¼ cup diced red bell pepper

One 8-ounce can tomato sauce

1 cup cream-style corn

2 tablespoons chili powder

1 tablespoon cumin powder

Salt and freshly ground black pepper

3 cups chunked precooked boneless, skinless chicken meat (1 pound)

One 4.5-ounce can chopped green chiles, drained

One 16-ounce can kidney beans, rinsed and drained

1 package Mexican-style cornbread mix

2 large eggs

⅔ cup milk

1. Preheat the oven to 400°F.

2. In a heavy skillet over medium-high heat, heat the oil. Add the onion,

garlic, and bell pepper and cook, stirring, until the onion is translucent and softened, about 3 minutes.

3. Add the tomato sauce, corn, chili powder, cumin, and salt and pepper to taste. Stir well. Cook for about 5 minutes.

4. Stir in the cooked chicken, green chiles, and beans. Cook until the mixture is hot.

5. Scrape the mixture into a casserole or baking dish and spread it out evenly.

6. In a mixing bowl, combine the cornbread mix with the eggs and milk. Pour it over the top of the casserole dish and bake in the oven for about 30 minutes, or until the mixture is hot and bubbly and the cornbread topping is golden brown.

*S*HORT-CUT TIPS

SUBSTITUTION: If you can't find Mexican cornbread mix in your supermarket, simply add some crushed red pepper flakes or chopped fresh jalapeños to a plain cornbread mix.

PLAN AHEAD: To freeze individual servings (mini pies), line the baking dishes with foil and bake as called for. Let them cool, freeze, then lift each pie out of its dish and foil, and pop them into individual freezer bags. They can easily be heated up in the microwave.

FRIDAY NIGHT BROWN BAG BAKED GARLIC CHICKEN

When we were growing up, my mother would put flour, salt and pepper, and whatever other seasonings she wanted into a brown paper bag. Then she'd put in the chicken and let us kids shake the bag until everything was well mixed together. It was an early lesson in how cooking in a bag makes for easy clean-up. You can use a

brown bag as I have in this recipe, and recycle those grocery bags that seem to
accumulate. Or use any number of the baking bags available from your supermarket.

MAKES 4 SERVINGS

One 3½- to 4-pound whole chicken

Olive oil

Salt and freshly ground black pepper

Paprika

Sprigs of fresh rosemary and thyme

2 medium onions, cut into large chunks

1 dozen small new red potatoes

4 carrots, cut into chunks

12 whole cloves garlic

½ cup chicken broth (fat-free optional)

1. Preheat the oven to 375°F.

2. Remove the giblets from the inside of the chicken. (You can freeze these for later use in stocks or dressing recipes.) Rinse the chicken and pat dry with paper towels.

3. Drizzle some olive oil over the outside skin of the chicken. Add salt and pepper to taste to both the inside and outside of the chicken. Sprinkle paprika over all.

4. Insert a few sprigs each of the rosemary and thyme inside the chicken. Add a few chunks of the onion.

5. Place the chicken in a roasting pan or casserole dish and scatter the remaining onions, potatoes, and carrots around the chicken in the pan. Sprinkle with the garlic cloves.

6. Add more salt and pepper to taste. Pour the broth into the pan.

7. Place the pan inside a large brown paper grocery bag. Fold the ends over and staple or pin them shut.

8. Place the pan on the center rack of the oven. *Make sure the rack is low enough so that the bag doesn't touch the top heating element, or else the bag will catch fire.* Bake for about 1½ hours.

9. Test doneness by cutting into the thickest part of the chicken breast. Juices should run clear and meat should be white. If necessary, place chicken back in the oven for another 20 to 30 minutes (although a chicken this size should be very well cooked in the given time).

10. Remove the pan from the oven. Cut the bag open with scissors. Let the chicken sit for at least 10 minutes before cutting it into pieces and serving.

11. Serve the chicken with vegetables and any pan juices.

SHORT-CUT TIPS

SUBSTITUTION: To make a parchment cooking bag quickly, use a long sheet of parchment paper, fold it in half, and staple down the sides to close it. You now have a bag to slip the chicken into.

PLAN AHEAD: Save the "giblets" from whole chickens. Either freeze them for use in other recipes or make a hearty chicken broth to freeze for later use.

PLAN AHEAD: Bake 2 chickens at a time to have enough cooked chicken for chicken salad, soups, or sandwiches. Cooked chicken meat can easily be frozen in plastic freezer bags.

RECIPE RESCUE: If you love garlic, but find the aftertaste too strong, reduce the strength of raw garlic by simmering it in water for 8 to 10 minutes before adding it to recipes.

TIME SAVER: Instead of peeling carrots and potatoes, just rinse them well and pat dry to remove any dirt. Add them to recipes as usual.

TOOL TIP: Terra-cotta roasters are a wonderful way to cook whole chickens.

GRILLED TEQUILA-LIME CHICKEN WITH SAVORY POLENTA AND SALSA

For an impromptu meal, here's a quick and easy chicken recipe inspired by the "Really Rich and Expensive Chicken" Robin Leach made on Country Kitchen. *I substituted tequila for his trademark champagne. If you prefer a nonalcoholic version, try using apple cider instead, and if it doesn't have enough "bite" for you, mix in a little cider vinegar!*

MAKES 4 SERVINGS

4 boneless, skinless chicken breasts (6 ounces each), rinsed and
   patted dry

2 fresh whole limes, cut in half

¼ cup tequila (or apple cider)

2 teaspoons paprika

Salt and freshly ground black pepper

1 package premade garlic-flavored polenta (from supermarket)

Unsalted butter

Fresh Corn and Black Bean Salsa (recipe on page 146) or your
   favorite store-bought salsa

Freshly grated Parmesan cheese for garnish

1. Prepare a gas, electric, or charcoal grill. Place the chicken breasts in a shallow glass bowl (a pie plate or baking dish will work).

2. Squeeze the lime juice over the chicken. Drizzle the tequila over the chicken.

3. Add paprika and salt and black pepper to taste. Cover and marinate for 10 minutes.

4. Remove the chicken from the marinade and grill it for 10 to 12 minutes on high heat, or until cooked throughout. (Note: You can also broil or pan-fry the chicken.) Remove from heat, set aside, and keep warm.

5. Slice the polenta into ¼-inch slices. In a skillet over medium-high heat, melt the butter. Fry the polenta slices for about 1 minute on each side, or until they are a crispy, golden brown. Place the slices in a single layer on a baking sheet in a warm oven until ready to serve.

6. To serve, place a chicken breast on each dinner plate.

7. Add the polenta slices and top them with salsa, either homemade or from the supermarket.

8. Sprinkle Parmesan over the top of the dish. Serve immediately.

SHORT-CUT TIPS

STEP SAVER: Prepared salsas of many varieties can be purchased in supermarkets. You can use them as they are, or add a few more ingredients to dress them up.

STORAGE TIP: To store hard cheese, like Parmesan, dampen a sheet of paper towel with cider vinegar and wrap it around the cheese to inhibit the growth of mold, then place the cheese in a plastic bag, seal it, and keep in the cheese compartment (the warmest place) in your refrigerator. Remoisten it every few days if necessary, and it should last for several weeks.

FRESH CORN AND BLACK BEAN SALSA

As a cilantro fan, I think salsa is a perfect accompaniment to a simple chicken dish. There are many wonderful prepared salsas available for speedy dinner preparation. But sometimes I like to make my own because, if they're in season, nothing beats fresh ingredients like tomatoes and corn. In the case of fresh jalapeños, discard the seeds, if you want to cut down on the heat. **MAKES 4 SERVINGS**

1 cup chopped fresh tomatoes (regular, Roma, or cherry in winter)

2 ears fresh corn, cooked 3 to 4 minutes in the microwave

One 15.5-ounce can black beans, rinsed and drained

2 tablespoons chopped fresh parsley

2 tablespoons chopped fresh cilantro

1 to 2 fresh jalapeño peppers, seeded and minced

2 tablespoons balsamic vinegar

Juice of 1 lime

Pinch of sugar

Salt and freshly ground black pepper

1. Place the chopped fresh tomatoes in a glass or nonreactive mixing bowl.

2. Cut the kernels from the 2 ears of cooked corn. Add to the bowl.

3. Stir in the black beans, parsley, and cilantro. Add the jalapeño, vinegar, lime juice, and sugar. Toss well.

4. Add salt and freshly ground black pepper to taste. Adjust the seasonings. Cover and refrigerate until ready to serve.

SHORT-CUT TIPS

SUBSTITUTION: There are many hot chile peppers available today for all your favorite hot recipes. Some of my favorites are the jalapeño, habanero, and serrano. You can also substitute hot dried chile peppers if fresh are not available.

MEASUREMENT SAVVY: Two medium ears of corn equal 1 cup kernels; 10 ounces frozen corn equal 1¾ cups kernels.

SANITY SAVER: To remove the remaining silk after removing the husk, rub a damp paper towel over the ear of corn, or use a damp, soft-bristle toothbrush.

SANITY SAVER: Take care when working with fresh, hot peppers. Use rubber or plastic gloves if your hands are sensitive. Either way, be sure to wash your hands well.

SHOPPING TIP: Look for jalapeños that have a firm skin and deep luscious colors with no shriveling.

SHOPPING TIP: Buy the freshest corn possible. Avoid corn sold with the husk removed—it's probably old, discolored, or wilted. Old corn will deteriorate faster and has less natural sweetness.

STORAGE TIP: Corn on the cob can be frozen for up to 3 months. Cover each ear in plastic wrap, then in aluminum foil. Don't unwrap until completely thawed.

SPICY AVOCADO-TOMATILLO SALSA

You can also use this salsa with the Grilled Tequila-Lime Chicken.

MAKES 4 SERVINGS

2 ripe tomatoes, chopped

2 ripe avocados, cored, peeled, and chopped

3 medium tomatillos, diced

1 small red onion, diced

1 bunch cilantro, chopped

½ cup plain yogurt or sour cream

3 cloves garlic, crushed and chopped

Hot pepper sauce

Juice of ½ lime

> **MINI:**
> PEPPER GARLAND—**for recipes and for kitchen decoration. If you can't use all your favorite chili peppers while they're fresh, simply string them through the stems with a needle and thread, creating a garland, and hang it up to dry—creating a quick and easy, useful decoration for your kitchen.**

1. In a large glass bowl, gently mix together the tomatoes, avocados, tomatillos, red onion, and cilantro.

2. Add the yogurt and garlic and mix gently but well.

3. Add hot pepper sauce and lime juice to taste. Toss well. Adjust seasonings. Cover and chill before using. This is great served with tortilla chips.

SHORT-CUT TIPS

INGREDIENT SAVVY: The two most commonly available avocado varieties are the Haas, which is almost black, and the Fuerte, which is larger and green with smooth skin.

SHOPPING TIP: Tomatillos are in the same family as the tomato. They have a tart, acidic taste that is complementary for use in salsas. Store them in the refrigerator in a brown paper bag for up to one month.

HERB AND NUT–ROASTED CORNISH HENS

This easy, elegant recipe was inspired by Barry Williams, who played my "son" Greg on The Brady Bunch. *Many years later he prepared delicious Cornish hens on my show,* Country Kitchen. *It was wonderful to see him as an adult, creating a romantic and sophisticated meal, and I was a very proud "mom"! This is a good recipe for a midweek dinner party where time is of the essence but you'd like to serve something delicious and visually impressive.*

MAKES 4 SERVINGS

6 cloves garlic

½ cup finely chopped pecans (or almonds, cashews, or hazelnuts)

½ teaspoon dried oregano

½ teaspoon dried thyme

½ teaspoon paprika

1 teaspoon dried rosemary leaves

Salt and freshly ground black pepper

¼ cup olive oil

2 Cornish hens, cut in half down the middle (to make 4 halves)

1. Preheat the oven to 400°F.

2. In the bowl of a food processor, mix together the garlic, pecans, oregano, thyme, paprika, and rosemary leaves. Pulse until the mixture is pastelike. Add salt and black pepper to taste. Pulse lightly a few times.

3. Drizzle in the olive oil and pulse briefly. Scrape the mixture into a small container.

4. Rinse and pat dry the hen halves. Place them, cut side down, in a large baking dish that has been covered with foil (for easy clean-up!).

5. Pat the pecan mixture over the tops of the hen halves. The mixture will be crumbly and will not really "stick" to the skin and fall to the sides in the pan.

6. Bake the chicken in the oven for 30 to 45 minutes, until the inside of the hens are cooked, and the outside is golden brown and crusty. (Increase the heat to the maximum, or broiler, setting for a few minutes if you would like the skin side crustier.) Serve hot with the crunchy pecan mixture from the pan.

*S*HORT-CUT TIPS

STEP SAVER: Use a large, sharp chef's knife to cut the hens down the middle, or get the butcher to cut them for you.

STEP SAVER: If you buy frozen Cornish hens, to thaw them properly immerse them in a bowl of cold water while they're still in their wrapping. Place this bowl in the refrigerator and leave until completely thawed.

GADGET SUBSTITUTION: If you don't have a food processor, use a mortar and pestle to blend the ingredients for the paste.

TURKEY HASH ON
SPICY CORNMEAL PANCAKES

After the holidays, we're always looking for creative ways to use the leftover turkey. My solution is to chop it up into small cubes and create a "hash," then serve it on top of some great pancakes. Since the meat is ready to use, this dish takes very little time, and gives the familiar turkey a new flavor and character. I call this "hash in a dash"!

MAKES 4 SERVINGS

2 tablespoons butter

2 tablespoons olive oil

1 cup raw diced potatoes (any type)

1 cup diced onion

2 ribs celery, chopped

2 cloves garlic, crushed

1 teaspoon paprika

Salt and freshly ground black pepper

1 cup chicken broth (low-fat optional)

1 cup water

2 cups cooked and chopped turkey meat (real turkey, not deli type)

½ cup light or heavy cream

Chopped fresh parsley for garnish

Cornmeal Pancakes (recipe on page 153)

1. In a stockpot over medium-high heat, melt the butter and olive oil together.
2. Add the potatoes, onion, celery, and garlic. Stir and cook until the onions and potatoes begin to soften, about 4 minutes.

3. Season the mixture with paprika and salt and pepper to taste.

4. Increase the heat to high. Pour in the broth and water and bring to a boil. Reduce the heat to medium-low and simmer until the potatoes are softened, 15 to 20 minutes. (Add more water if necessary as the liquid cooks off.)

5. Add the chopped turkey and heat thoroughly.

6. Add the cream and garnish with parsley. Heat well and serve immediately or keep warm until ready to serve. Serve over the Cornmeal Pancakes.

---

*S*HORT-CUT TIPS

SUBSTITUTION: If you don't have cream to enrich the broth, just mix together ½ cup milk plus 2 tablespoons butter.

TIME SAVER: To have cooked turkey really fast, buy a boneless, skinless turkey tenderloin. Cook it in the microwave until the juices run clear, about 8 to 10 minutes. Chop and add it to recipes as called for.

CORNMEAL PANCAKES

Since these pancakes feature hush puppy mix, which is already flavored with spices, you'll save preparation time.

MAKES 4 SERVINGS (ABOUT 2 PANCAKES PER PERSON)

Vegetable oil

½ cup freshly grated Parmesan cheese

Dash of hot pepper sauce

1 box hush puppy mix, prepared according to package directions (or
  use a regular cornbread mix)

1. In a skillet over medium-high heat, heat 2 tablespoons of the vegetable oil.

2. While the skillet is heating, stir the cheese and pepper sauce into the prepared hush puppy mix.

3. Pour ¼ cup of the mixture at a time into the hot skillet and cook each cornmeal pancake for 1 to 2 minutes on each side, or until golden brown. Add more oil as needed. Repeat until all the mixture is cooked. Once they are cooked, place the pancakes on a baking sheet in a warm oven, uncovered, until you're ready to serve them.

*S*HORT-CUT TIPS

SUBSTITUTION: If you can find only cornbread mix, to give it the same flavor as the hush puppy mix, add some black pepper, onion salt, and garlic powder. If desired, use vegetable cooking spray to fry these pancakes.

SUBSTITUTION: Use Swiss or Monterey Jack cheese instead of Parmesan. Try adding corn niblets or minced scallions.

SHOPPING TIP: Look for hush puppy mix in the fish section of your supermarket. These mixes usually just need some water to prepare. Other ingredients can be added to spice them up.

TURKEY MEAT LOAF

A meat loaf of any kind always reminds me of home and what I call a basic comfort food. Use ground beef, pork, veal, or chicken for the turkey if desired. You can even mix two of these meats together for a very special and unique meat loaf. My own modern version of the classic is perfect to serve with mashed potatoes. The leftovers also make great cold sandwiches the next day.

MAKES 6 TO 8 SERVINGS

1 cup unflavored dry bread crumbs

2 large eggs

½ green bell pepper, chopped

1 medium onion, chopped

2 cloves garlic, crushed

One 4.5-ounce can mild green chiles, drained and chopped

1 teaspoon dried oregano

1 teaspoon dried thyme

Dash of cayenne pepper

1 teaspoon ground cumin

¼ cup ketchup

2 pounds ground turkey

2 tablespoons chopped fresh parsley

Salt and freshly ground black pepper

MINI:

QUICK AND EASY MEAT LOAF SANDWICHES: **Mix up this recipe and press equal portions of the mixture into muffin tin cups. Bake in a 375°F oven for 20 to 25 minutes, until cooked through. Let cool, cover, and freeze. Store the individual mini meat loaves in plastic freezer bags and use them as desired for meat loaf sandwiches or as individual servings. Reheat in a 375°F oven until thawed and heated through to serve.**

1. Preheat the oven to 350°F, and have ready a loaf pan or 9-by-5-inch baking dish.

2. Place the bread crumbs in a large bowl and add the eggs. Toss the mixture well.

3. Add the bell pepper, onion, garlic, and chiles and mix well.

4. Stir in the oregano, thyme, cayenne, and cumin and mix well. Add the ketchup and mix well again.

5. Work the ground turkey into the dry ingredients, preferably with your hands! (You can use a spoon, but your hands will make quick work and you'll have a much better consistency to your meat loaf. You can always use plastic gloves if you like.)

6. Sprinkle the chopped parsley, salt, and black pepper to taste over the mixture and mix well.

7. Press the meat loaf mixture firmly into a loaf pan. Bake in the oven for about 45 minutes, or until the center is no longer pink. If the top begins to brown too much before the meat loaf is cooked inside, place a sheet of aluminum foil loosely over the top.

8. Remove the meat loaf from the oven, and let it sit for about 10 minutes before slicing.

*S*HORT-CUT TIPS

TIME SAVER: Make quick bread crumbs in your food processor using slightly stale (or lightly toasted) bread. Or crush very dry bread slices in a plastic freezer bag with a rolling pin.

SANITY SAVER: Use a meat loaf pan with drip holes in its bottom to drain off fatty juices.

MESS SAVER: Mix up the entire recipe in a large resealable plastic bag. Simply add all the ingredients and work them together with your hands. No muss, no fuss!

TURKEY AND
BLACK BEAN ENCHILADAS

Believe it or not, this has replaced one of my favorite foods—the cheeseburger! Many years ago when I lived in New York with my sister Emily, we existed for months eating nothing but simple foods like burgers. This recipe uses traditional Tex-Mex ingredients, with turkey replacing the ground beef because it's so light. But I still love cheese, as you can see!

MAKES 4 TO 6 SERVINGS

12 small corn tortillas (approximately 6 inches in diameter)

2 cups diced cooked turkey meat (real turkey meat, not deli style)

One 15.5-ounce can black beans, rinsed, well drained, and mashed

One 10-ounce package frozen chopped spinach, thawed and well drained

2 cups shredded Monterey Jack cheese

4 scallions, chopped

1 tablespoon ground cumin

One 8-ounce package cream cheese, softened

One 4-ounce can diced green chile peppers, well drained

1 cup canned enchilada sauce for serving

Sour cream for serving

1. Preheat the oven to 375°F. Spray a 9-by-13-inch baking pan with nonstick cooking spray. Wrap the tortillas in foil and place them in the warm oven.

2. In a mixing bowl, combine the turkey meat, mashed black beans, spinach, 1 cup of the cheese, scallions, cumin, softened cream cheese, and diced chile peppers. Blend well.

3. Spoon some of the turkey mixture down the center of each tortilla. Roll the tortilla around the filling. Place the filled tortilla, seam side down, in the baking dish.

4. Drizzle enchilada sauce over the top of the enchiladas and sprinkle on the remaining cup of Monterey Jack cheese.

5. Cover the baking dish with foil and place it in the oven. Bake the enchiladas for about 30 minutes, or until hot. Remove the foil for the last 7 to 8 minutes of cooking time to brown the top lightly. Serve hot with your favorite enchilada sauce (or salsa) and sour cream, if desired.

*S*HORT-CUT TIPS

MEASURING SAVVY: If your recipe calls for a specific-sized pan or baking dish but you're unsure of the dimensions of yours and don't have a ruler or tape measurer handy, here's a trick. Use a dollar bill to measure your pan—all U.S. bills are exactly 6 inches long (or 3 folded in half)!

PLAN AHEAD: Assemble extra enchiladas, freeze in plastic freezer bags, and reheat some other time for a quick dinner.

MEAT

Sometimes when you're planning a holiday meal or picnic, nothing else suits the occasion but a meat dish! My pal Dom DeLuise always offers to carve the meat so he can nibble while doing so, while moaning with delight. I think his greatest short-cut is knowing how to eat quickly! As this collection of recipes shows, I like to combine meat with fruit whenever possible. There are endless delicious meat-and-fruit combinations, and you can use the fruit to create portions that only seem large, but are still light. A little meat goes a long way. And using less meat means you're saving money too!

Whether it's beef with mushrooms, peanuts, or cherries, or pork with applesauce or cranberries, or lamb with apricot or tangerine relish, most of my favorite meat dishes make great leftovers, and can be enjoyed in some form way beyond their first appearance!

It's always a challenge to keep the kitchen clean and bacteria free when you're working with meat, particularly counters. Here's a suggestion. Mix a few tablespoons of bleach with a cup of water and put the solution in a spray bottle. Spritz the mixture on a sponge or directly onto the counter surface and rub down. You can also throw the sponge in the dishwasher or put it in the microwave for a minute to clean.

STIR-FRIED BEEF AND SHIITAKE MUSHROOMS

Stir-frying is one of the quickest cooking methods, and it's perfect for thin strips of meat like the flank steak in this recipe. For a more tender meat, slice the steak across the grain. If you don't have mushrooms, any colorful vegetables will work, such as zucchini, yellow squash, or green bell peppers. It's a great dish to serve over rice-flour noodles, which are very thin and require only a few minutes of cooking time. Look for them in your supermarket in the Asian food section, or in an Asian market.

MAKES 4 SERVINGS

1 pound flank steak, trimmed of fat and cut into strips about 4 inches long and ¼ inch thick

2 tablespoons soy sauce

½ cup rice wine

1 tablespoon sesame oil

3 tablespoons vegetable oil

4 whole scallions, each cut into 2-inch pieces

3 cloves garlic, crushed

6 to 8 ounces shiitake mushrooms, sliced (discard the stems)

1 generous tablespoon minced fresh ginger

Dash of crushed red pepper flakes

1. Place the strips of steak in a glass bowl and add the soy sauce, ¼ cup of the rice wine, and the sesame oil. Let the meat marinate for about 15 minutes, stirring occasionally. (Note: You can do this step in the morning before going to work and let the meat sit, covered, in the refrigerator until later in the day.)

2. Heat a wok or wok-type skillet over high heat, until very hot. Drizzle 1 tablespoon of the vegetable oil into the hot wok and swirl it around to coat the sides.

3. Add the flank steak strips and cook, stirring constantly, until the pink disappears from the meat. Remove the meat from the wok and set aside.

4. Reduce the heat to medium-high. Add another tablespoon of vegetable oil to the wok and swirl. Scatter the scallions and the garlic into the wok and cook, stirring constantly, for a few seconds.

5. Add the last tablespoon of vegetable oil and the mushrooms to the wok. Cook, stirring constantly, until they begin to soften, about 3 minutes.

6. Drizzle the remaining ¼ cup of rice wine over the mushrooms and continue to cook, stirring, for about 3 minutes more.

7. Return the cooked steak to the wok and scatter the minced ginger and red pepper flakes over all. Drizzle any of the leftover marinade mixture over the meat. Cook, stirring, for 3 to 4 minutes, or just until the liquid comes to a simmer.

8. To serve, drizzle extra soy sauce over the stir-fry as desired.

*S*HORT-CUT TIPS

TOOL TIP: If you don't have a real wok for this recipe, a skillet will work, too.

SANITY SAVER: When stir-frying, add the slowest-cooking ingredient first and the fastest-cooking last. Stir constantly.

SANITY SAVER: For an easier job and thinner slices, freeze the meat for this recipe for about 30 minutes before slicing.

SANITY SAVER: To test that the heat of your pan is sufficient, insert a whole scallion into the hot oil. It should sizzle!

ZESTY CURRIED BEEF AND
PEANUTS OVER BASMATI RICE

I love the combination of flavors in this dish, especially the curry, which I enjoyed so much when I visited India. Buy precooked roast beef from your supermarket deli for this recipe, or the next time you cook a roast, cook extra and freeze some for this and use in other recipes. The basmati rice takes 20 to 25 minutes to cook, but the end result is well worth the time. The preparation for this recipe is actually quick, and you can accomplish other tasks while it cooks. Serve it with the Pear-Apple Chutney for an authentic Indian dish.

MAKES 4 SERVINGS

2 tablespoons peanut oil

1 medium yellow onion, chopped

½ red bell pepper, cut into slivers

2 cloves garlic, chopped

1 generous teaspoon curry powder, or more to taste

½ teaspoon crushed red pepper flakes

1 tablespoon cornstarch mixed with ¼ cup orange juice

½ cup orange juice

2 cups chunked precooked lean beef steak

½ cup toasted lightly salted peanuts (page 44)

Freshly ground black pepper

2 to 3 cups hot cooked basmati rice, prepared according to package
   instructions

Peach-Apple Chutney (recipe on page 164) or your favorite premade
   chutney

1. In a large skillet over medium-high heat, heat the peanut oil.

2. Add the onion, bell pepper, and garlic. Cook, stirring, until the onion is transparent and softened, 3 to 4 minutes.

3. Stir in the curry powder and pepper flakes. Cook for approximately 1 minute.

4. Pour in the cornstarch–orange juice mixture and blend well. Add the ½ cup orange juice. Stir until thickened and hot.

5. Stir in the cooked beef and peanuts and heat thoroughly. Season to taste with black pepper.

6. Serve the mixture over the rice with the chutney on the side.

SHORT-CUT TIPS

SUBSTITUTION: If you don't have curry powder on hand, make your own using any combination of turmeric, crushed red pepper flakes, cumin, nutmeg, white pepper, cardamom, and ginger. Use a coffee grinder for a fine blend. Experiment!

SUBSTITUTION: If you can find quinoa in your market, it's a highly nutritional, wonderful, and versatile grain to use as a cereal, for a salad base, or in a dish like this one.

RECIPE RESCUE: If you have only salted peanuts and you're trying to cut down your salt intake, simply rinse the peanuts in a colander under cold water and pat them dry. Use in recipes as directed.

TIME SAVER: Cooked rice freezes beautifully, so whenever you cook it, make extra to freeze in plastic bags. Just thaw and heat in the microwave, and it's ready to eat.

SANITY SAVER: When you're measuring liquids, don't try to hold the measuring cup steady. For an accurate measure, fill the cup and place it on a level counter. Then get down to eye level to check the measure.

PEACH-APPLE CHUTNEY

Cook this recipe uncovered so excess liquid evaporates and the chutney will thicken. Chutney can be made a day or two ahead and stored in the refrigerator in a covered jar. It's wonderful with curries! **MAKES ABOUT 4 CUPS**

> 3 ripe but firm peaches (or nectarines), halved and pitted, coarsely chopped
>
> 2 Granny Smith apples (or other tart apples), cored and coarsely chopped
>
> ½ cup currants or regular dark raisins
>
> ½ cup golden raisins
>
> ¾ cup rice vinegar or white wine vinegar
>
> ¼ cup apple cider vinegar
>
> ½ cup dark or light brown sugar
>
> 2 tablespoons minced fresh ginger
>
> 1 teaspoon yellow or brown mustard seeds
>
> ½ teaspoon ground cinnamon

1. In a saucepan over medium-high heat, combine all the ingredients. Stir together gently.

2. Bring the mixture to a boil, then lower the heat to medium-low and simmer, stirring occasionally, until the fruit is softened, 15 to 20 minutes. Serve warm or cold.

SHORT-CUT TIPS

RECIPE RESCUE: If your raisins or currants have dried out, don't throw them away. You can easily plump them up for recipes by soaking them in hot tea. This adds back the flavor lost when they dried out.

SANITY SAVER: Vinegar is volatile and therefore loses pungency when heated. If you prefer the acidity of vinegar, stir it into the recipe after the dish has been removed from the heat.

STORAGE TIP: Once a box of raisins has been opened, it should be stored in an airtight container and refrigerated. Properly stored, raisins are good for up to two years. They can also be stored in the freezer in a tightly sealed plastic bag for up to a year, and will thaw quickly at room temperature.

STEAK AU POIVRE WITH DRIED CHERRIES

*This dish is a favorite since I love to put pepper (*poivre*) on almost everything! This combination of beef and fruit is delicious, and it's a snap to put together. Most pepper mills or grinders have adjustable settings so that peppercorns can be ground from very fine to very coarse. For this French classic, adjust your pepper grinder to coarse and use fresh peppercorns to rub into the meat.*

MAKES 4 SERVINGS

1 cup chicken broth (fat-free optional)

½ cup orange juice

½ cup cranberry juice

1 cup dried cherries

2 tablespoons light or dark brown sugar

Salt

4 beef steaks (your favorite, about 6 to 8
    ounces each); if large, use 2 steaks
    cut into 2 pieces each

2 tablespoons cracked black pepper

1 tablespoon olive oil

¼ cup brandy (or apple juice)

1 teaspoon fresh rosemary leaves

> **MINI:**
>
> To dry rosemary, place the stems of fresh rosemary on a wire cooling rack and place it in a warm oven (lowest possible setting) overnight. When the rosemary is dry, place it in jars with tight-fitting lids to store.

1. In a saucepan over medium heat, combine the broth, orange juice, cranberry juice, dried cherries, brown sugar, and salt to taste. Cook until the mixture is reduced by half, 5 to 8 minutes.

2. While the broth mixture is cooking, press the cracked pepper into both sides of the steaks. Press hard so it will stick to the surface of the meat.

3. In a nonstick skillet over medium-high heat, heat the oil. Cook all of the steaks until browned on both sides and done to your liking. This will take about 2 to 3 minutes on each side for rare steaks, and longer for medium or well done.

4. Remove the steaks to a warm plate. Add the brandy to the skillet and cook until the mixture is reduced by half, 3 to 5 minutes. Sprinkle the rosemary leaves into the pan and stir for a few seconds.

5. Add the dried cherry mixture to the pan and cook until the sauce is thickened somewhat, about 5 minutes. Adjust the seasonings and add salt to taste.

6. To serve, place a pool of sauce on each dinner plate and lay the steaks on top of each. Serve immediately.

> **MINI:**
>
> Make your own cracked pepper blends. Buy and experiment with a variety of peppercorns and grind them together in a pepper grinder. Some of my favorites are the classic black peppercorn, like Tellicherry and Lampong. Less pungent is the white peppercorn. Green, pink, and Szechuan peppercorns are also wonderful.

*S*HORT-CUT TIPS

TOOL TIP: To make a quick funnel to simplify filling your pepper grinder, cut a paper envelope in half diagonally. Snip off one corner, open it up, and pour the pepper through your paper funnel.

HOUSEHOLD HINT: If you spill wine on a tablecloth, cover it with a mound of salt. When dry, just brush it away. The salt absorbs the wine completely.

QUICK SEARED STEAK WITH ONIONS

Searing meat over high heat is a great cooking technique because it develops flavor and color by browning the surface of the meat, creating something of a crust, while the inside of the meat remains juicy. You need a heavy skillet for this process, and you need it very hot! It's one of the quicker ways to cook a steak, especially when paired with another quick-cooking ingredient like onions!

MAKES 4 SERVINGS

2 tablespoons olive oil

2 medium red onions (or sweet yellow like Vidalia), cut into slivers

4 sirloin strip steaks (or your favorite steak cuts), 1 inch thick (6 to 8 ounces each)

Salt and freshly ground black pepper

1. Preheat an iron skillet (or other heavy skillet) over medium-high heat. When hot, add the olive oil and swirl it around to coat the sides.

2. Add the onions and cook, stirring often, until golden brown, 5 to 7 minutes. Reduce the heat to medium-low and continue to cook the onions for about 10 minutes, until they start to caramelize. Remove the onions from the skillet and set aside.

3. Season the steaks with salt and pepper to taste. Increase the heat to medium-high, and when the skillet is very hot, add the steaks. Quickly sear the steaks on both sides and continue cooking them until the inside of the steaks are to your liking, 6 to 8 minutes for rare, or longer for well done. When the steaks are cooked, add the onions back to the skillet and continue to cook until well heated. Serve the steak and onions immediately.

SHORT-CUT TIPS

SANITY SAVER: Don't salt the meat until just before cooking because salted steak will dry out if it sits too long.

STEAK AND SHRIMP KEBABS WITH PEANUT SAUCE

Barbara Eden, star of I Dream of Jeannie, *once made me a traditional lamb kebab that I loved. My recipe has a different combination of ingredients, yet her cooking tips work just as well for my quick "meal on a stick"! For instance, placing lemon wedges on skewers between meat or seafood heats the lemon and makes it easier to squeeze the juice out. It also makes a great presentation! If you use pineapple juice in this recipe instead of wine, it's good to have individual-portion-sized cans of juice on hand, so there's no leftover juice to go to waste.*

MAKES 4 SERVINGS

PEANUT SAUCE

2 tablespoons lemon juice

2 tablespoons soy sauce

½ cup creamy or chunky peanut butter

3 to 4 cloves garlic, crushed

1 tablespoon chopped fresh ginger

1 tablespoon light or dark brown sugar

¼ teaspoon crushed red pepper flakes

1 tablespoon olive oil

½ cup orange juice

Salt and freshly ground black pepper to taste

KEBABS

1 pound tenderloin, rinsed and patted dry, cut into 1½-inch cubes

2 dozen large shrimp, peeled, tails left on, rinsed and patted dry

4 lemons, cut into wedges

¼ cup soy sauce

¼ cup white wine (or pineapple juice)

1 clove garlic, minced

Freshly ground black pepper

Dash of cayenne pepper or hot pepper sauce

2 teaspoons fresh rosemary, or 1 teaspoon dried

1. To make the peanut sauce, in a blender or food processor, combine the lemon juice and soy sauce. Blend well.

2. Add the remaining sauce ingredients. Blend the mixture until smooth. Adjust the seasonings to taste.

3. To make the kebabs, preheat the broiler or grill.

4. Place the steak cubes, shrimp, and lemon wedges in a large glass or nonreactive mixing bowl.

5. Add the soy sauce, wine, garlic, black pepper to taste, cayenne, and rosemary. Toss together well.

6. Presoak wooden skewers in water for 30 minutes to keep them from burning up on the grill. Thread, alternating the steak, shrimp, and a lemon wedge, onto metal or wooden skewers. You will need 2 skewers per person.

7. Place the skewers on the grill or under the broiler and cook for 4 to 5 minutes, then turn and cook for 4 to 5 minutes more. The shrimp should be thoroughly cooked, and the steak will be barely rare on the inside. While the kebabs are cooking, baste with any leftover juices in the mixing bowl.

8. When the kebabs are done, remove them from the grill and cover with foil to keep them from drying out. Place in a warm oven until ready to serve. Serve with the peanut sauce on a bed of your favorite rice.

$\mathcal{S}$HORT-CUT TIPS

INGREDIENT SAVVY: Raw shrimp are usually easier to peel and devein than cooked.

RECIPE RESCUE: When olive oil is refrigerated, it can become cloudy and too thick to pour. To reliquefy it, allow it to stand at room temperature. To speed the process, place the sealed bottle in a bowl of hot water.

TOOL TIP: You can use natural rosemary and sage stems from your garden as skewers—they flavor the food and look great. Remove the leaves from sturdy stems and then cut one end into a point. Thread the ingredients to be grilled onto the stems.

STORAGE TIP: Rinse fresh, uncooked shrimp under cold running water and drain thoroughly. Refrigerate, tightly covered, for about 2 days. Shrimp can be frozen, tightly covered, for up to about 3 months, then thawed overnight in the refrigerator.

FAVORITE BEEF STROGANOFF

This recipe reminds me of the days when I thought beef Stroganoff was a fancy dish. When I first arrived in New York, I was intimidated by the foreign-sounding name, but of course I learned that beef Stroganoff uses simple ingredients and is easy to prepare. Now I make my own, updating the classic with ingredients like wild mushrooms or crème fraîche, wine, and capers. But whichever way I make it, it's a family favorite. Try this same recipe with pork, veal, lamb, or chicken.

MAKES 6 SERVINGS

¾ cup sour cream

1 tablespoon Dijon-style mustard

1½ tablespoons tomato paste

2 tablespoons chopped sun-dried tomatoes packed in oil

2 tablespoons capers, rinsed and drained (optional)

2 tablespoons Worcestershire sauce

2 teaspoons paprika

½ to 1 cup white wine (or orange juice)

Salt and freshly ground black pepper

¼ cup (½ stick) unsalted butter

1 medium yellow onion, cut into slivers

1½ pounds beef tenderloin, cut into strips

8 ounces fresh wild mushrooms (or white button mushrooms), cut in
    bite-sized pieces

Cooked egg noodles

Chopped fresh parsley

1. In a bowl, combine the sour cream, mustard, tomato paste, sun-dried tomatoes, capers, Worcestershire sauce, paprika, wine, and salt and black pepper to taste. Whisk together well. Set aside.

2. In a large skillet over medium-high heat, melt the butter. Add the onion and cook, stirring, until it's translucent, about 3 minutes. Reduce the heat to medium.

3. Add the tenderloin strips and cook, stirring, until cooked through, about 5 minutes.

4. Add the mushrooms and cook, stirring, for 3 to 4 minutes.

5. Reduce the heat to medium-low. Add the sour cream mixture to the pan and toss the ingredients together well. Cover and cook until the Stroganoff is hot, about 5 minutes.

6. Serve over the hot egg noodles and sprinkle with parsley.

SHORT-CUT TIPS

TIME SAVER: If you have some leftover canned tomato paste, freeze it in ice cube trays. Pop the frozen tomato paste cubes into a resealable plastic freezer bag, and keep frozen until needed. Each cube will be about a tablespoon.

SANITY SAVER: Look for tomato paste in reclosable tubes, which can be found in large supermarkets and specialty groceries. When a recipe like this one calls for only a few tablespoons, squeeze out the desired amount, then reclose the tube for later use.

MESS SAVER: Cut sun-dried tomatoes directly into recipes or measuring cups using scissors. No cutting board clean-up! Also use kitchen scissors to cut parsley.

SHOPPING TIP: Wild mushrooms are available in most large supermarkets. When purchasing, look for mushrooms that are firm and dry.

SIMPLE SUNDAY SUPPER POT ROAST

My dad made the best pot roast, and I think he'd be pleased with his daughter's easy-to-prepare recipe. It just pops into the oven to cook with no fuss and no muss. I call it a "smart supper," since the leftovers can last into the following week. Roast beef sandwiches, vegetable beef soup, and roast beef hash are just a few of the great quick meals that can be made with the leftovers. Thanks, Dad, for starting a great tradition!

MAKES 6 SERVINGS (OR TWO WITH LOTS OF LEFTOVERS TO WORK WITH)

One 4-pound chuck or bottom round roast (or rump or brisket), rinsed and patted dry

3 cloves garlic, crushed

½ cup flour seasoned with salt, black pepper, paprika, and chopped fresh parsley

3 tablespoons good-quality olive oil

1 bag baby carrots (about 24 carrots)

4 Yukon Gold potatoes, unpeeled, quartered

1 bunch scallions, trimmed and cut into 4 sections

2 ribs celery, chopped

1 cup beef or vegetable broth

1 cup white wine (or substitute nonalcoholic wine or additional broth)

2 bay leaves

1. Preheat the oven to 350°F.

2. Rub the outside of the roast with the crushed garlic. Shake the seasoned flour over the roast, turning to coat it all well.

3. In a large roasting pan over medium-high heat on top of the stove, heat the olive oil.

4. Add the roast to the roasting pan and cook, turning on all sides, until it is golden brown. Remove the pan from the stove and turn the heat off.

5. Scatter the carrots, potatoes, scallions, and celery around and over the roast in the pan.

6. Pour the broth and wine around the roast and add the bay leaves.

7. Cover the roasting pan with a lid, or aluminum foil, and bake in the oven for 1½ to 2 hours. Cut into the meat to check doneness. Remove the cover and bake for another 30 minutes.

8. Remove the bay leaves and serve slices or chunks of the roast with vegetables and pot juices. It's wonderful served with some crusty bread to mop up the juices.

SHORT-CUT TIPS

TIME SAVER: Use precut frozen vegetables when in a real hurry.

TIME SAVER: To flavor a frozen roast, remember it's easier to rub fresh garlic onto a frozen roast than onto a thawed one. The rough surface actually grates the garlic as you rub. As it thaws, the essence of the garlic soaks into it.

SANITY SAVER: To add bay leaves to a recipe like pot roast, put them in a tea ball or cheesecloth so they can be removed easily without fishing around for them.

SANITY SAVER: If your cooking oil hasn't been used in a while, make sure to taste or smell it before use, to determine if it has become rancid. The smallest bit of spoiled oil can ruin a dish.

HOUSEHOLD HINT: To remove candle drippings from table linens, place a bag of ice on top of the wax. When the wax hardens, peel off as much as possible. Then turn the fabric over and place on top of a paper towel blotter. Press the area with a warm iron until the wax is absorbed by the paper towel.

SPICY BARBECUE JERK RIBS

I was on a television show with Jerry Mathers, "The Beav" of Leave It to Beaver. *The grown-up Jerry turned out to be quite a cook. He made his "Favorite Ribs," a big hit with the cast and crew. My recipe differs from his, but for added flavor, you might add his secret ingredient to the sauce—½ cup of dark beer!*

MAKES 4 SERVINGS

1 small onion, chopped

¼ cup lemon juice

2 tablespoons olive oil

1 jalapeño pepper, cored, seeded, and minced

2 tablespoons molasses (any type)

2 tablespoons ketchup

Dash of hot pepper sauce

4 cloves garlic, chopped

1 teaspoon dried thyme

1 teaspoon ground nutmeg

2 teaspoons chopped fresh ginger

2 tablespoons light or dark brown sugar

Salt and freshly ground black pepper

10 bay leaves

3 to 4 pounds pork spareribs or Southern-style short ribs

1. In a glass mixing bowl, combine the onion, lemon juice, olive oil, jalapeño, molasses, ketchup, hot pepper sauce, and garlic. Blend together well.

2. Stir in the thyme, nutmeg, ginger, brown sugar, and salt and black pepper to taste.

3. Sprinkle the bay leaves into the mixture and gently mix.

4. Place the ribs in a large plastic bag and pour in the barbecue jerk sauce. Close the bag and place it in the refrigerator for a few hours or overnight.

5. When ready to cook, preheat the grill or broiler.

6. Remove the ribs from the marinade and place them on the grill or in the broiler pan under the broiler. Grill or broil for 7 to 8 minutes on one side, then turn the ribs and cook for another 4 to 5 minutes on the other side. The ribs should be browned and their surface should be just beginning to char.

7. Pour any leftover sauce from the plastic bag into a small saucepan. Simmer over medium-low heat for 10 minutes while the ribs are cooking.

8. While they're cooking, baste the ribs with the sauce a few times. Serve the ribs hot.

SHORT-CUT TIPS

INGREDIENT SAVVY: Spareribs are the most popular ribs for barbecuing. They're quite fatty, which makes them very tasty when cooked. Short ribs generally have more meat on them than spareribs and are equally wonderful when cooked.

SANITY SAVER: To prevent sticking, oil the grill rack or broiler pan before adding the meat.

SANITY SAVER: To measure molasses, use the same utensil (unwashed) used to measure the olive oil, and the molasses will slide off instead of clinging to the utensil.

CITRUS GRILLED PORK CHOPS WITH EASY ORANGE APPLESAUCE

When you need an unusual flavor combination for an outdoor gathering, here's an easy dish to grill. I've suggested pork loin chops because they cook quickly, but you can use any of your favorite cuts. The natural sugar in the citrus, soy, and honey combine to form a glaze and make a wonderful presentation. You can prepare the marinade in the morning before you leave for work, and have it ready to go when you return at night. When topped with the accompanying applesauce recipe, this is a perfect sweet-and-sour experience.

MAKES 4 SERVINGS

1 orange

2 tablespoons lemon juice

1 tablespoon soy or tamari sauce

1 teaspoon dried thyme

2 cloves garlic, crushed

Salt and freshly ground black pepper

¼ cup olive oil

2 tablespoons honey

4 pork loin chops, 1 inch thick (6 ounces each), rinsed and patted dry

Easy Orange Applesauce (recipe on page 180)

1. Remove the zest from the orange with a vegetable peeler or citrus zester, being careful not to cut into the pith (white part). Place the zest in a food processor and chop finely. Place the chopped rind in a glass bowl.

2. Cut the orange in half and squeeze the juice from both halves into the bowl with the rind.

3. Add the lemon juice, soy or tamari sauce, thyme, garlic, and salt and pepper to taste; mix.

4. Whisk in the olive oil and honey.

5. Place the chops in this marinade. Let them sit for at least 30 minutes. (This step can be done the previous day or the morning of, stored in the refrigerator.)

6. Heat the grill or broiler. Remove the chops from the marinade and place them on the grill or on the broiler pan under the broiler.

7. Baste the chops with the marinade while cooking. Cook for 5 to 6 minutes, then turn the chops over and cook for another 5 minutes. The chops should be well done in the center. Top with the Orange Applesauce.

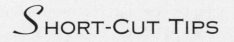

SHORT-CUT TIPS

TOOL TIP: Don't spend a lot of money for basting brushes. Buy paintbrushes at your local hardware or home center store. Wonderful and inexpensive pure bristle brushes with natural, unfinished handles are available in a variety of sizes for much less than those sold in kitchenware stores.

MESS SAVER: Save a lot of clean-up by marinating the chops in a resealable plastic bag. Just add everything to the bag, close, and wait!

GADGET SUBSTITUTION: Use your vegetable peeler or citrus zester to remove the peel from oranges. Grating on a box grater won't give you very pretty-looking peel, and you can easily nick your fingers.

EASY ORANGE APPLESAUCE

This is a quickie sauce to make for any grilled dish. Although I prefer apples, if you like, you can make an "easy pear sauce" using fresh ripe pears instead.

MAKES 4 SERVINGS, WITH EXTRA FOR LEFTOVERS

4 tart apples, halved, cored, and cut into large chunks

2 oranges, peeled, seeded, and cut into sections

½ cup cranberry juice

Juice of 1 lemon

¼ cup sugar

1 teaspoon ground cinnamon

1. Place all of the ingredients in a saucepan. Cook over medium-high heat until the mixture begins to bubble. Reduce the heat to low, cover, and cook for 12 to 15 minutes. Stir and coarsely mash the apples with the back of a wooden spoon. Cook for another 5 minutes. The mixture should be chunky, but very soft.

2. Cool the mixture to room temperature. Serve with pork chops or refrigerate until ready to use.

SHORT-CUT TIPS

TIME SAVER: If you're in a really big hurry, just open a can of Mandarin oranges, rinse, and drain. Then add to the recipe with the other ingredients.

HOUSEHOLD HINT: Whenever you peel citrus fruit, don't throw the peel away. Save it for use in other recipes or even to make potpourris. It's very easy to dry or freeze.

To dry peel: Cut the peel from the fruit and place the pieces on a baking sheet in a 200°F oven. Check the peels at half-hour intervals, and remove when dried. The time will vary depending on what types of peels you are drying. Chop the dried peels in a food processor and store in a jar with an airtight lid, or in a plastic bag.

To freeze peel: Cut the peel from the fruit, chop it, and put it in a resealable plastic freezer bag. Press out as much air from the bag as possible, then seal and freeze.

APRICOT LAMB CHOPS AND NUTTY COUSCOUS

I once did a video project with Shari Lewis and her puppet Lamb Chop, which involved writing and performing one-minute stories from the Bible. The next time I worked with Shari and Lamb Chop was on the set of Country Kitchen *with a lamb recipe. The engaging Lamb Chop suggested we use beef, but Shari prevailed. She knew that lamb chops cook quickly since they tend to be small, and Lamb Chop knew better than to argue with her "creator"! There you have the "genesis" of this recipe, which is sweetened by apricots, and combines nicely with Nutty Couscous.*

MAKES 4 SERVINGS

2 tablespoons olive oil

8 lamb chops (2 per person since they're usually small),

    rinsed and patted dry

½ cup apricot jam

¼ cup chopped dried apricots

½ cup apple juice

Salt and freshly ground black pepper

Nutty Couscous (recipe opposite)

1. In a skillet over medium-high heat, heat the olive oil. Add the lamb chops and cook until golden brown on both sides. Reduce the heat to medium-low, and cook for 5 to 6 minutes.

2. In a small bowl, combine the apricot jam, dried apricots, and apple juice. Blend together well.

3. Pour the jam mixture over the chops in the skillet. Cover and cook for about 10 minutes. Add the salt and pepper to taste.

4. To serve, place 2 chops on each dinner plate and drizzle some of the apricot sauce from the pan over each. Serve with the couscous as a side dish.

*S*HORT-CUT TIPS

SUBSTITUTION: Instead of apple juice, try cranberry juice, red or white wine, or grape juice.

SANITY SAVER: To make dried apricots even easier to cut, first place them in the freezer for about 30 minutes.

MESS SAVER: You can easily cut dried fruit with scissors directly into a measuring cup. Rub a little oil on the scissors blades to keep the fruit from sticking. Or dip the blades of the scissors in hot water frequently.

NUTTY COUSCOUS

Couscous, a granular semolina, is a staple of North African cooking. To cook, just bring the liquid to a boil, add the couscous, then remove it from the heat. Cover and let it stand in the hot liquid until it's absorbed. It's one of the easiest side dishes you can make and great as a base for salads or with any number of meats or vegetables.

MAKES 4 SERVINGS

1½ cups plain couscous

1 cup chicken broth (fat-free optional)

1 cup water

½ cup chopped toasted nuts (page 44)—pecans, walnuts, pine nuts, hazelnuts, almonds—a mixture of your favorites

2 generous tablespoons chopped fresh parsley

1. Cook the couscous according to the package directions, using the chicken broth and the water as the cooking liquid.

2. To the cooked couscous, add the nut mixture and the chopped parsley. Toss together well. Serve the couscous hot, as a side dish with lamb, fish, or chicken.

SHORT-CUT TIPS

SUBSTITUTION: In addition to water and chicken broth, try cooking couscous in vegetable broth or apple or orange juice. These add a delicious flavor to the couscous.

SUBSTITUTION: Prepare the couscous by lining a metal sieve with a piece of cheesecloth. Place the sieve over a pot of boiling water. Add the couscous and cover. Steam until it's fluffy and cooked.

SMOKED HAM AND
THREE-CHEESE CALZONE

You can use any of your favorite cheeses for this recipe. If you buy all or most of it preshredded, you'll save lots of time and energy. In fact, another name for this recipe might be "Wham Bam Ham," since just about every ingredient can be bought prepackaged and ready to use!

MAKES 4 SERVINGS

1 cup ricotta cheese

1 teaspoon dried Italian seasoning

1 cup freshly grated Gruyère cheese

¼ cup freshly grated Parmesan cheese

1 cup chopped smoked ham (from deli section of grocery)

Salt and freshly ground black pepper

One 10-ounce package ready-to-bake pizza dough (from refrigerator
   section of grocery)

1. Preheat the oven to 425°F. Lightly spray a pizza pan or baking sheet
   with nonstick cooking spray.

2. In a mixing bowl, combine the ricotta cheese, Italian herbs, Gruyère
   and Parmesan cheeses, and ham. Stir together well. Add the salt and
   pepper to taste.

3. Place the pizza dough on the prepared pan and, working from the
   center out, pat the dough into a 12- to 14-inch circle.

4. Spread the ham and cheese mixture onto half of the circle of dough,
   leaving a 1-inch border.

5. Wet the edges of the bottom half of the crust with water. Fold the dough over the filling and press the top and bottom together firmly. Press the edges with the tines of a fork to seal firmly.

6. With a sharp knife, cut a few slits in the top of the dough to allow steam to escape while baking.

7. Bake in the oven for 20 to 25 minutes, until golden brown and the inside is bubbly. Remove from the oven and cool slightly on a rack. Cut it into 4 equal pieces and serve it hot.

---

*S*HORT-CUT TIPS

PLAN AHEAD: Prepare the calzone and freeze it to cook later. Or make small, individual calzone as appetizers and freeze before baking. Use your favorite ingredients as fillings: sun-dried tomatoes, spinach, pine nuts—the list is endless.

TIME SAVER: You can purchase refrigerator or frozen pizza dough to use for this type of recipe. The refrigerator pizza dough comes in a tube, like biscuits. When you open and unroll the dough, try not to overwork it, which toughens it.

PORK TENDERLOIN WITH CRANBERRY RELISH

Holiday time means "hustle" time for most of us, so it's important to have reliable recipe short-cuts that leave us with more time to spend with family and friends. By using a smaller cut of meat like the tenderloin instead of a roast, you can reduce cooking time by almost a third. This recipe uses a combination of traditional flavors,

but makes use of packaged and prepared products as much as possible. In fact, you
can even use canned cranberry sauce for the fresh whole cranberries.

MAKES 6 SERVINGS

3 cups fresh or frozen whole cranberries

1 orange, peeled, seeded, and coarsely chopped

½ cup packed light or dark brown sugar

¼ cup cranberry juice (or apple, grape, orange)

1 tablespoon olive oil

One 2- to 2½-pound pork tenderloin, rinsed and patted dry, cut into
1½-inch-thick slices

Salt and freshly ground black pepper

Slivers of fresh garlic

¼ cup white wine (or white grape juice)

1. In a small saucepan, mix together the cranberries, orange, sugar, and cranberry juice.

2. Over medium-high heat, bring the mixture to a boil. Reduce the heat to medium-low and simmer until the cranberries pop, about 8 minutes. Remove the saucepan from the heat and set aside.

3. In a skillet over medium heat, heat the oil.

4. Using a sharp knife, make a few slits in the surface of each slice of pork. Gently rub salt and pepper into the surface of each piece.

5. Insert a sliver of fresh garlic into each cut. Press the garlic into the meat.

6. Cook the tenderloin pieces in the hot oil until they're golden brown, 6 to 8 minutes, then turn and cook for 6 to 8 minutes more. Occasionally, press the pieces firmly down into the pan with a spatula. Remove the cooked pork from the pan. The juices of the meat should run clear. Set the pork aside, covered, to keep warm until ready to serve.

7. Increase the heat under the skillet to medium-high and add the wine. Scrape the pan with a wooden spoon to deglaze.

8. Add the cranberry mixture to the pan and heat it for 2 to 3 minutes. Stir often.

9. To serve, place a "pool" of cranberry-orange sauce on each plate and top with 2 slices of pork.

SHORT-CUT TIPS

MEASUREMENT SAVVY: One 12-ounce bag of whole cranberries equals about 3 cups, or about 2½ cups finely chopped.

PLAN AHEAD: Fresh cranberries may be in season for only a short time in your area, so buy some extra and freeze them for future use.

RECIPE RESCUE: To neutralize some of the cranberry's natural acidity, add ¼ teaspoon baking soda while cooking, and you'll need to use less sugar.

HOUSEHOLD HINT: To clean silver quickly before company arrives, grab a tube of toothpaste! Use it just like a commercial silver cleaner. Apply it with a soft sponge and gently rub the tarnish away. Then rinse it well. Any type of toothpaste will do—gel or plain—and it even works on silver jewelry (great for travel)!

HOUSEHOLD HINT: For extra multipurpose measuring cups, take plain, clear drinking glasses and mark on each ¼-, ½-, ¾-, and 1-cup measures. Use a store-bought measuring cup and water to determine where to place measurement marks with an indelible pen.

PASTA AND ONE-DISH WONDERS

One of the fastest ways to get a meal on the table is to make a "one-dish" menu, greatly reducing preparation time, the number of utensils needed, and clean-up time. Whether you're single, serving a family, or rushing to feed a crowd, this is a great way to cook! Pastas, casseroles, pizzas, and paella are versatile and satisfying since they include a wide range of vegetables, poultry, meat, and fish.

Like a lot of entertainers, I love to eat pasta because it's nutritious and not especially fattening if you watch what you put on it. There were probably more pasta recipes prepared on *Country Kitchen* than anything else. One guest, singer B. J. Thomas, told me that he liked to inhale the steam when he uncovered the pasta pot because it opened up his throat for singing. So do I. There may be more professional ways to vocalize, but none nearly as delicious!

SUN-DRIED TOMATO PASTA WITH FRESH VEGETABLES

My son Joseph, an enthusiastic runner, always made a huge bowl of pasta for extra energy before he ran. This prompted me to try different ways to prepare pasta, whether to encourage his athletic aspirations or just to enjoy. One result is this dish, a colorful mélange of red, green, and yellow which goes well with grilled chicken, fish, or pork. I just made this up one day with what was in the kitchen. It's now one of my staples.

MAKES 4 TO 6 SERVINGS

1 tablespoon butter (or nonstick cooking spray)

1 pound fresh asparagus, cut into ½-inch pieces

1 yellow bell pepper, cored, seeded, and coarsely chopped

1 orange bell pepper, cored, seeded, and coarsely chopped

1 lemon, halved and seeded (for juice)

Freshly ground black pepper

1 teaspoon dried Italian seasoning

½ cup chicken broth (fat-free optional)

1 pound sun-dried tomato linguine (or plain linguine), cooked until al dente

½ cup freshly grated Parmesan cheese

> ## MINI:
>
> **My son Joseph's recipe for pasta is simply a little butter or olive oil, Parmesan cheese, and Tabasco sauce, with pasta cooked al dente.**

1. In a large skillet over medium-high heat, melt the butter.

2. Add the asparagus and bell peppers. Cook, stirring, just until the vegetables begin to soften, about 5 minutes.

3. Squeeze the lemon juice over the vegetables and toss together well. Sprinkle over all the freshly ground black pepper to taste and the Italian seasoning.

4. Drizzle the chicken broth over the vegetables and reduce the heat to low. Cover and simmer for about 5 minutes more.

5. Remove the cover and add the cooked pasta. Toss until well mixed. Adjust the seasonings to taste.

6. Serve with shredded Parmesan cheese over the top.

SHORT-CUT TIPS

SUBSTITUTION: In a pinch, use bottled lemon juice instead of fresh. Use lemon to replace salt flavor in foods, or to keep vegetables a bright color.

TIME SAVER: Fresh pastas cook in less time than dried. Keep an eye out for fresh pastas in your supermarket.

TIME SAVER: If you happen to have a chunk of Parmesan or even Romano cheese, don't take time to grate it for this easy recipe. Simply use a vegetable peeler to create "flakes" or "slivers" of cheese to top this great dish.

PASTA PANCAKES WITH FRESH TOMATO-BASIL SAUCE

When Ben Vereen made tomato-basil pasta for us on Country Kitchen, *he signed his recipe, "Life is good." I couldn't resist his philosophy or his sauce, and so I created a version of Ben's sauce for my own pasta dishes. This recipe is both an easy and delicious way to use leftover pasta.*

MAKES 6 SERVINGS

PANCAKES

½ pound cooked vermicelli or angel-hair pasta, broken into 2-inch
  pieces before cooking

2 large eggs, slightly beaten

Salt and freshly ground black pepper

1 tablespoon chopped fresh parsley

Olive oil (for frying pancakes)

SAUCE

2 tablespoons olive oil

2 cloves garlic, minced

Two 14.5-ounce cans diced or stewed tomatoes, drained

1 medium bunch fresh basil, leaves torn into pieces (or chopped)

Salt and freshly ground black pepper

Crumbled goat cheese (chèvre) for garnish

1. To make the pancakes, place the well-drained, cooked pasta in a mixing bowl. Add the eggs, salt and pepper to taste, and the fresh parsley. Mix well.

2. In a nonstick skillet over medium heat, drizzle a small amount of the olive oil.

3. Place about ¼ cup of the pasta-egg mixture in the hot skillet and gently spread it out with a spatula until it's somewhat thin. Cook for 1 to 2 minutes, until the pancake is golden brown on the first side. Flip it over and cook until the other side is golden, 1 to 2 minutes. Repeat with the remaining pasta mixture.

4. When the pancakes are cooked, place them on a baking sheet in a warm oven. Don't layer or cover them, since this will cause them to lose their crispness. Keep warm until they're ready to serve.

5. To make the sauce, in a skillet over medium-high heat, heat the olive oil. When the oil is hot, add the garlic and cook until it has softened, about 1 minute.

6. Stir in the tomatoes. Scatter the basil and salt and pepper to taste over the tomatoes. Reduce the heat to medium-low and cook until the sauce is hot. Adjust the seasoning to taste.

7. To serve, place 2 pancakes on the bottom of each dinner plate and top them with the hot sauce and crumbled goat cheese.

---

*S*HORT-CUT TIPS

SERVING TIP: For a dramatic presentation, use this same recipe to make 1 large pancake in a skillet. Brown it as called for, then cut it into wedges to serve.

SANITY SAVER: To keep the edges from turning black, tear fresh basil into pieces with your fingers instead of cutting it with a knife. The black edges don't show when basil is cooked, but they don't look good in salads.

LEMON PASTA WITH ALMONDS

This is truly a last-minute meal to whip up for unexpected company. It's the simplest way I know to dress up a plain dish and create a distinctive and tasty dinner. If you keep a few flavored pastas and packaged toppings in your pantry, you'll always be a few time-saving steps ahead. This recipe features the light flavor combination of lemon and almonds, but depending on your own tastes, the possibilities for combination are endless.

One 12- to 16-ounce package lemon-flavored fresh pasta (linguine or fettuccine)

1 tablespoon olive oil, preferably extra-virgin

Salt and freshly ground black pepper

½ cup toasted chopped almonds (page 44)

¼ cup crumbled feta cheese

1. Cook the pasta according to the package directions until al dente. Remove the pasta from the water and drain well.

2. Toss the pasta in a warm bowl with the olive oil, salt and pepper to taste, and the almonds.

3. Sprinkle with the crumbled feta cheese. Toss well. Serve hot.

MINI:

If your supermarket doesn't have lemon pasta, make your own by adding a bit of lemon zest to plain pasta after it has cooked. Toss well.

Another delicious combination to add to cooked pasta is a little crisp bacon and watercress, tossed with olive oil or butter.

SHORT-CUT TIPS

SANITY SAVER: To keep pasta hot longer when serving, warm the bowl first. Just fill it with hot water, let it stand for 5 minutes, empty the water, and add the pasta. Or, if the bowl is microwave-safe, heat it on high in the microwave until warmed, 2 to 3 minutes.

LASAGNA ROLLS FLORENTINE

Florentine means "in the style of Florence, Italy," but my name has nothing to do with my appreciation for this dish! I love everything about that glorious city. Today, the cooking term usually refers to dishes with eggs and spinach, two ingredients that are easy to find, store, and use. "Florentine" dishes are often sprinkled with cheese when served, which is how I enjoy mine.

MAKES 4 SERVINGS

2 whole large eggs, lightly beaten

Two 10-ounce packages frozen spinach, thawed and well drained

1 cup ricotta cheese

1 cup shredded or grated mozzarella cheese

½ cup freshly grated Parmesan cheese, plus extra for garnish

1 tablespoon minced garlic

Salt and freshly ground black pepper

¼ teaspoon ground nutmeg

8 to 10 lasagna noodles, cooked al dente (regular or a flavored type)

2 to 3 cups good-quality tomato-based jarred pasta sauce

1. Preheat the oven to 375°F.

2. In a mixing bowl, combine the eggs, spinach, ricotta, mozzarella, Parmesan cheese, garlic, salt and pepper to taste, and nutmeg. Blend together well.

3. Lay the cooked lasagna noodles out one at a time on a sheet of wax paper. Pat dry with paper towels.

4. Spread about ¼ cup of the filling mixture on each noodle, spreading it evenly. Leave about ½ inch of noodle uncovered at each end.

5. Roll up each noodle around the filling. (Secure with a toothpick if necessary.) Place the lasagna rolls, seam side down and not touching, in a baking pan.

6. Pour the pasta sauce over the rolls. Cover the pan loosely with foil and bake it in the oven until the lasagna rolls are heated throughout. Remove any toothpicks, if used.

7. Serve 2 rolls per person, with sauce and a sprinkling of additional Parmesan.

SHORT-CUT TIPS

PLAN AHEAD: Make the noodle rolls ahead of time and freeze if desired. Or make extra when you have time, store them in plastic freezer bags, and pull them out of the freezer when you're in a hurry. Thaw in the microwave according to your microwave's instructions. Preheat the oven to 375°F. When thawed, place the noodle rolls in the baking pan, add some pasta sauce, and bake for 10 to 15 minutes, until hot and bubbly.

SHOPPING TIP: Most large supermarkets carry many kinds of flavored lasagna, such as spinach and sun-dried tomato.

Seafood Lasagna

Many years ago the delightful and irrepressible comedian Henny Youngman served me a seafood and pasta dish that he called "Take My Recipe, Please!" Well, I did, and added a few of my favorite ingredients. It's a rich dish, but worth the splurge. Now, if only I could add the right one-liners and play the violin! Well, I'm sure Henny and Jack Benny are now sharing laughs with my friend George Burns—so I'll dedicate this recipe to those wonderful gentlemen!

MAKES 4 TO 6 SERVINGS

2 tablespoons olive oil

1 small red onion, chopped

One 8-ounce package cream cheese, softened

One 15-ounce container ricotta cheese

1 tablespoon dried Italian seasoning

Salt and freshly ground black pepper

1 large egg, lightly beaten

One 10.75-ounce can cream of mushroom soup

One 10.75-ounce can cream of shrimp bisque or soup

¼ cup white wine (or white grape juice)

1 pound cooked, peeled small shrimp

½ pound cooked crabmeat

½ cup grated Parmesan cheese

9 lasagna noodles, cooked according to package directions

1 cup shredded mozzarella cheese

1. Preheat the oven to 350°F if cooking immediately. Or assemble the ingredients and refrigerate until ready to cook.

2. Add the olive oil to a skillet over medium heat, and cook the onions until they are softened, about 5 minutes. Reduce the heat to medium-low.

3. Add the cream cheese, ricotta, Italian seasoning, and salt and pepper to taste. Stir until well mixed and creamy. Remove the skillet from the heat and stir in the egg. Set aside.

4. In a bowl, mix together the mushroom soup, shrimp bisque, white wine, shrimp, crabmeat, and Parmesan cheese.

5. Layer 3 noodles in the bottom of a 9-by-13-inch casserole or a baking dish. Layer on half of the soup mixture and half of the cheese mixture. Top with 3 more noodles and the remaining soup mixture and the cheese mixture. Top with the remaining noodles.

6. Scatter the mozzarella cheese over the top. Cover loosely with foil and bake in the oven until the lasagna becomes hot and bubbly, 35 to 40 minutes. Uncover for the final 5 minutes of cooking time. Let the lasagna stand at room temperature for about 15 minutes before serving.

---

*S*HORT-CUT TIPS

SUBSTITUTION: To make yogurt cheese as a substitute for ricotta cheese in this recipe, put 2 cups of plain nonfat yogurt into a cheesecloth-lined strainer, and place it over a bowl. Refrigerate, covered, overnight or for at least 5 hours. The longer the yogurt is strained, the firmer the cheese will be. Use yogurt cheese as you would ricotta.

TOMATO TART

Another one of my favorite brown-bag lunches is this savory tart, which can be cut into wedges or squares. If you like it hot, reheat it in the microwave. If you're a tomato lover like I am, you'll really go for this.

MAKES 6 SERVINGS

¼ cup freshly grated Parmesan cheese

½ cup shredded mozzarella cheese

One 9-inch frozen pie shell, thawed according to package

    directions

1 generous teaspoon dried Italian seasoning

¼ cup minced onion

¼ cup chopped sun-dried tomatoes (use oil-packed type, drained)

4 to 6 Roma tomatoes, sliced into circles and patted dry

½ cup half-and-half

3 large eggs

2 tablespoons chopped fresh parsley

Salt and freshly ground black pepper

1. Preheat the oven to 350°F.

2. Sprinkle the Parmesan cheese and ¼ cup of the mozzarella cheese over the bottom and slightly up the sides of the pie shell. Shake the Italian seasoning evenly over the cheeses.

3. Scatter the minced onion and chopped sun-dried tomatoes over the pie shell.

4. Overlap the Roma tomato slices in a circular pattern over the other ingredients.

5. In a measuring cup or small bowl, mix together the half-and-half, eggs, chopped parsley, and salt and pepper to taste.

6. Slowly pour the egg mixture into the pie shell. Gently tap the pie pan on a counter surface to get rid of air bubbles and to help the egg mixture seep down into the pie.

7. Sprinkle the remaining ¼ cup of mozzarella cheese over the top.

8. Place the pie pan on a baking sheet pan and bake in the oven until the custard is set, 35 to 40 minutes. Let cool on a rack. Cut the tart into wedges and wrap individually for lunches.

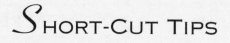

*S*HORT-CUT TIPS

SANITY SAVER: Use a jar with a lid to mix liquids such as the half-and-half custard ingredients in this recipe.

STORAGE TIP: Let the tart cool completely, then slice it and wrap each slice in plastic wrap. Place in a plastic bag or wrap in foil and you have a lunch you can grab on the run.

STORAGE TIP: To pack your lunchbox successfully so items don't get smashed, put heavier items in the bottom of the bag or box, and the lighter items on top. Lunch will be much more pleasant. If you take your lunch to work on a regular basis, buy small individual-portion plastic boxes to use especially for this purpose. Also, a lunch-sized cooler is an excellent way to keep sandwiches in better shape.

STORAGE TIP: Always wrap pickles and tomato slices separately in plastic so they don't make a soggy mess. Add them to sandwiches when you're ready to eat.

Quick and Easy Vegetable and Cheese Frittata

A frittata, or Italian omelette, is one of my favorite breakfast meals to serve houseguests. It also makes a wonderful light lunch served with a small salad. You can cook it ahead of time and serve at room temperature. And it's basically a one-dish meal, so clean-up is easy. Feel free to experiment with this recipe, because almost any vegetables can be included.

MAKES 6 SERVINGS

3 tablespoons unsalted butter

12 large eggs, lightly beaten with ¼ cup half-and-half

Salt and freshly ground black pepper

One 10-ounce package frozen spinach, thawed and well drained

One 8.5-ounce can artichoke hearts, drained and chopped

2 red bell peppers, roasted (page 107), drained, and sliced

2 tablespoons chopped fresh parsley

½ cup freshly grated Parmesan cheese

1. Preheat the oven to 425°F.

2. In a 12-inch oven-safe skillet (with an oven-proof handle) over medium heat, melt the butter.

3. Add the eggs. Cook, stirring, until they're barely soft-scrambled, about 1 minute. The eggs should be very runny and not at all set. Remove the skillet from the heat. Season with salt and pepper to taste.

4. Sprinkle the spinach evenly over the eggs.

5. Scatter the artichoke hearts, roasted bell peppers, and parsley over all. Sprinkle with the Parmesan cheese.

6. Bake in the oven for about 10 minutes, or until the edges of the omelette are lightly browned and the cheese is melted. To serve, cut into wedges.

Huevos Rancheros Burritos

I first became interested in burritos because my son Robert has always loved them and ate them with any kind of filling. This is a great breakfast or brunch recipe for a crowd and the ingredients can easily be doubled or tripled based on the number of guests. I find that 1 burrito per person is usually sufficient. You can prepare the burritos up to 3 months in advance and freeze them. If you don't have black beans, use any canned beans—kidney, pinto, or even white beans are terrific!

MAKES 8 SERVINGS

RANCHERO SAUCE

2 tablespoons olive oil

1 red bell pepper, cored, seeded, and chopped

2 teaspoons minced garlic

Two 4.5-ounce cans chopped green chiles

Pinch of sugar

1 tablespoon chili powder

1 teaspoon ground cumin

One 12-ounce jar of your favorite chunky tomato salsa

2 tablespoons balsamic vinegar

Two 15.5-ounce cans black beans, rinsed and drained

1 cup grated Monterey Jack cheese

½ cup grated sharp Cheddar cheese

1 teaspoon chili powder

1 teaspoon ground cumin

EGGS

16 large eggs

8 ounces cream cheese, cut into small chunks

Salt and freshly ground black pepper

1 package of large flour tortillas (approximately 8½ inches)

1. To prepare the ranchero sauce, in a large skillet over medium-high heat, heat the olive oil. Add the red bell pepper, garlic, and chiles. Cook, stirring, until the pepper is softened, 3 to 4 minutes.

2. Reduce the heat to medium. Stir in the sugar, chili powder, cumin, and salsa. Cook for about 5 minutes. Remove from the heat. Add the balsamic vinegar. Stir together well and set aside.

3. To prepare the beans, in a mixing bowl combine the black beans, Monterey Jack and Cheddar cheeses, chili powder, and ground cumin. Mix well. Set aside.

4. To prepare the eggs, crack them into a mixing bowl and lightly whisk.

5. Spray a large nonstick skillet with nonstick cooking spray and preheat it over medium heat. When the skillet is hot, pour in the eggs and cook them halfway, stirring often, about 1 minute.

6. Scatter cream cheese chunks over the eggs and stir in gently. Let the eggs cook until they're soft-scrambled or to your liking. Season them to taste with salt and pepper. Set aside.

7. To assemble the burritos, if cooking immediately, preheat the oven to 350°F. Lightly oil a baking dish.

8. For each burrito, lay 1 tortilla out on a flat surface. Place some of the bean mixture and scrambled eggs in the center of each.

9. Fold the tortilla up, burrito style, and place it in the prepared baking dish. Repeat the process until all the filling is used. (Note: At this point, you can continue and bake, or freeze the burritos to cook later.)

10. Top the burritos with ranchero sauce and bake in the oven until they're hot and bubbly, 30 to 35 minutes. Serve hot.

---

*S*HORT-CUT TIPS

SERVING TIP: For a party, use the smaller flour tortillas and make individual, smaller bite-sized burritos!

TIME SAVER: You can break this dish down into quick meal packs to pull from the freezer and microwave at the last minute.

TIME SAVERS: Be sure to buy preshredded Cheddar cheese to save on time. If in a hurry, just use a jarred salsa, and skip the additional ingredients called for to make the ranchero sauce.

You can also buy precut chiles in jars to save time, as well as minced garlic in a jar.

HOUSEHOLD HINT: Oil and water don't mix! The fiery sensation of chile peppers is due to a compound called capsaicin, which is an oil. That's why drinking water doesn't remedy the burning sensation. Nor will a beer or a margarita, since alcohol increases the absorption of the capsaicin. Instead, eat oil-absorbing, starchy foods like bread, rice, or potatoes, and bananas, as well as dairy products like milk, yogurt, or ice cream.

HERBED POTATO GALETTE

I grew up on fried potatoes and onions, and still love this dish, as most people seem to. But I've sampled a lot of interesting potato dishes since then, so here's my updated version, which is like a cross between fried and scalloped. It's a quick dish, since all the ingredients go in one skillet, and I don't spend time peeling the potatoes because the skins are so nutritious. Unlike other galettes, this one is not flipped over, which therefore saves a step! This is a great brunch dish to serve with scrambled eggs.

MAKES 6 TO 8 SERVINGS

2 to 2½ pounds potatoes, unpeeled

½ cup (1 stick) unsalted butter

2 teaspoons rosemary leaves

¼ cup chopped fresh Italian parsley

1 teaspoon paprika

1 teaspoon dried thyme

Salt and freshly ground black pepper

¾ cup freshly grated Romano cheese

¼ cup light or heavy cream mixed with
    ¼ cup chicken broth (fat-free
    optional)

> **MINI:**
> EASY SOUR CREAM TOPPING: **Mix together 1 cup sour cream (or plain yogurt) and herbs or minced vegetables such as scallions, carrots, or any of your choice. Serve with wedges of the galette.**

1. Preheat the oven to 400°F.

2. Wash and dry the potatoes. Slice thin.

3. In a 10-inch nonstick skillet over medium heat, melt 2 tablespoons of the butter. Swirl the butter around to coat the bottom of the pan. Remove from the heat.

4. Arrange a third of the potatoes in a spiral pattern on the bottom of the skillet. Overlap and cover the bottom of the skillet.

5. Cut 2 more tablespoons of butter into dots and sprinkle over the potatoes. Sprinkle some of the rosemary, parsley, paprika, thyme, salt and pepper to taste, and ¼ cup of the Romano cheese over all.

6. Continue layering the potatoes, butter, seasonings, and cheese to create 2 more layers. Press the layers down together gently.

7. Pour the cream-broth mixture over all the layers. Sprinkle the top with 1 tablespoon of chopped parsley.

8. Place the skillet, loosely covered with foil, in the oven and bake until the potatoes are soft, 30 to 40 minutes. Remove the foil and continue to bake until the top of the galette is golden brown.

9. Remove the skillet from the oven and let it stand for about 10 minutes before serving in wedges.

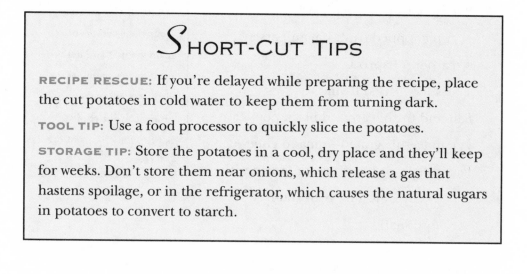

SHORT-CUT TIPS

RECIPE RESCUE: If you're delayed while preparing the recipe, place the cut potatoes in cold water to keep them from turning dark.

TOOL TIP: Use a food processor to quickly slice the potatoes.

STORAGE TIP: Store the potatoes in a cool, dry place and they'll keep for weeks. Don't store them near onions, which release a gas that hastens spoilage, or in the refrigerator, which causes the natural sugars in potatoes to convert to starch.

SPINACH AND GOAT CHEESE PIZZA

Ann B. Davis, or Alice on The Brady Bunch, *one of the dearest and most professional ladies I've ever worked with, shared my concern about feeding our families properly while we spent long hours together on the series. One of her secrets for getting a nutritious meal on the table fast was to make a great pizza! For a little pizzazz, my recipe adds goat cheese, a pure white goat's milk cheese with a wonderfully tart flavor that will perk up any pizza. Store the cheese, tightly wrapped, in the refrigerator for up to 2 weeks.*

MAKES 6 TO 8 SERVINGS

Olive oil

Coarse cornmeal

Premade pizza dough (thawed if frozen)

½ cup shredded mozzarella cheese

½ cup freshly grated Parmesan cheese

One 10-ounce package frozen spinach, thawed and well drained

1 medium red onion, slivered and cooked in microwave until
    translucent, about 1 minute

2 red bell peppers, roasted (use jarred or canned), coarsely chopped

2 cloves garlic, minced

6 ounces goat cheese, crumbled

¼ cup toasted pine nuts (page 44)

1 generous teaspoon dried Italian seasoning

2 tablespoons black olive paste

1 tablespoon capers, rinsed and drained

1. Preheat the oven to 425°F.

2. Lightly coat a 12-inch pizza pan with olive oil and sprinkle it with cornmeal.

3. Arrange the pizza dough over the pan, crimping it along the outer edge.

4. Cover the surface of the dough with ¼ cup of the mozzarella cheese and ¼ cup of the Parmesan cheese.

5. Arrange the spinach evenly over the cheese.

6. Sprinkle the cooked red onion slivers, roasted peppers, and garlic over all.

7. Sprinkle the goat cheese and pine nuts evenly over the vegetables. Shake the dried Italian seasoning over all.

8. Dollop the black olive paste over the pizza, and sprinkle the capers evenly over all.

9. Cover the top of the pizza with the remaining ¼ cup of mozzarella and ¼ cup of Parmesan.

10. Bake the pizza in the oven until it is hot and bubbly and the outer crust is golden brown, about 20 minutes.

---

*S*HORT-CUT TIPS

TIME SAVER: Buy frozen vegetables or precut vegetables from the produce area or salad bar of your market to make preparing this recipe quick and easy.

TIME SAVER: Precooking the onion in the microwave is easy, but you can skip that step if you don't mind the stronger onion flavor.

SANITY SAVER: To determine the accuracy of your oven temperature, invest in an inexpensive oven thermometer, and place it in the center rack of your oven. Set the oven to a desired temperature and, after 15 minutes, check to see if it agrees with the thermometer. If not, adjust the oven setting to match whenever you use the oven.

BLACK OLIVE PASTE

Black olive paste, or olivada, is now readily available in most larger supermarkets, but you can quickly make your own. Keep extra in a jar in the refrigerator for use in recipes. **MAKES 1¼ TO 1½ CUPS**

1 cup pitted black olives (Kalamata or other imported black olives)

2 cloves garlic, crushed

1 tablespoon capers, rinsed and drained

¼ to ⅓ cup olive oil, preferably extra-virgin

2 tablespoons chopped fresh parsley

1. Put the olives, garlic, and capers in a food processor fitted with a metal blade. Process for a few seconds until coarsely chopped.

2. With the processor running, drizzle the olive oil through the feed tube. Process until smooth.

3. Add the parsley and pulse a few times until well combined. Store in a jar with a tight-fitting lid in the refrigerator, for up to 2 months.

EASY STOVE-TOP RATATOUILLE

This is one of my favorite easy after-work recipes. I particularly love this in the summer when vegetables are fresh from the garden or local produce place. Use any leftovers for sandwiches or as a pasta topping. Like the rest of us who improve with age, this mixture gets better after a couple of days!

MAKES 4 TO 6 SERVINGS

2 tablespoons olive oil

3 to 4 cloves garlic, crushed

2 medium yellow onions, chopped

1 medium eggplant, cut into 1-inch chunks

4 zucchini, cut into chunks

1 green bell pepper, cored, seeded, and cut into chunks

One 14.5-ounce can Italian-style tomatoes, coarsely chopped

2 tablespoons balsamic vinegar

½ cup halved pitted black olives

2 teaspoons dried Italian seasoning

Salt and freshly ground black pepper

½ cup freshly grated Parmesan cheese

1. In large pot over medium heat, heat the olive oil. Add the garlic and onions. Cook, stirring, until the onions are transparent, 4 to 5 minutes.

2. Add the eggplant and cook, stirring, for 2 to 3 minutes. Stir in the zucchini, bell pepper, and tomatoes and cook, stirring, for 5 minutes more.

3. Add the balsamic vinegar, olives, Italian seasoning, and the salt and black pepper to taste. Reduce the heat to medium-low and stir well. Cover and cook until the vegetables are softened, about 5 minutes more.

4. Top the hot servings of ratatouille with Parmesan cheese.

---

*S*HORT-CUT TIPS

INGREDIENT SAVVY: When buying eggplant, choose a firm, smooth-skinned eggplant that seems heavy for its size. The skin on smaller, younger eggplants is edible. Larger eggplants should usually be peeled.

RECIPE RESCUE: Larger eggplants may be bitter. To remove the bitterness, cut them into slices and place in a colander. Sprinkle with salt. Let drain for about 30 minutes over a bowl or in the sink. Rinse and pat dry.

SHOPPING TIP: There are a number of types of eggplants currently available in most larger supermarkets and Asian markets. Look for Japanese or oriental eggplant, baby eggplant, or even white eggplant. Any of these will be delicious in this recipe.

VEGETABLE PAELLA

The first time I tasted paella was many years ago while performing at one of Puerto Rico's beautiful hotels. Since then, I've always enjoyed this one-dish meal made with seafood, as it's traditionally served in Spain. But when some friends said they preferred vegetables, I developed this recipe as a nice change of pace. You can use the vegetables I've recommended, or any of your personal favorites. Using canned and prepared items really cuts down the work. This is great with crusty bread!

MAKES 6 SERVINGS

2 tablespoons olive oil

1 red onion, chopped

2 medium carrots, peeled, cut into ½-inch pieces (or use baby carrots)

2 cups broccoli florets

2 cups cauliflower florets

1 red bell pepper, cored and cut into slivers

4 cloves garlic, crushed

1½ cups yellow saffron rice (one 10-ounce package)

2 cups chicken broth (fat-free optional) or vegetable broth

One 28-ounce can whole tomatoes, chopped

One 15-ounce can chickpeas, rinsed and drained

2 tablespoons capers, rinsed and drained

2 teaspoons minced fresh thyme, or 1 teaspoon dried

Salt and freshly ground black pepper

1. Preheat the oven to 375°F.

2. In a large nonstick oven-proof skillet over medium heat, heat the olive oil.

3. Add the onion, carrots, broccoli, cauliflower, bell pepper, and garlic. Cook, stirring often, until the vegetables are slightly softened, about 8 minutes.

4. Add the rice. Cook, stirring, for about 2 minutes. Add the chicken broth and tomatoes with their juice. Mix well.

5. Stir in the chickpeas, capers, thyme, and salt and pepper to taste. Remove the skillet from the heat and cover it.

6. Place the skillet in the oven and bake the paella for about 15 minutes, or until the rice is tender. Let stand at room temperature for about 10 minutes before serving.

SHORT-CUT TIPS

TIME SAVERS: Bags of preprepped cauliflower and broccoli can be bought in the produce section of large supermarkets.

Baby carrots from bags can be added "as is" to this recipe, with no cutting necessary.

MESS SAVER: Cut fresh herbs with scissors directly into recipes.

Chunky Tuna and Vegetable Casserole

Casseroles have always been one of the most popular one-dish meals for a very good reason—they're truly easy to put together and cook up fast. This one is a contemporary version of the '50s classic—it uses packaged items like canned tuna and water chestnuts for even greater speed. What a life-saver for working parents who have to juggle it all.

MAKES 6 TO 8 SERVINGS

2 tablespoons unsalted butter

1 cup chopped fresh mushrooms (regular or wild)

2 cups milk

3 tablespoons flour

2 cups chicken broth (preferably low-fat)

½ teaspoon *each* paprika, cayenne pepper, dried Italian seasoning, and grated nutmeg

Salt and freshly ground black pepper

One 9-ounce can white tuna, packed in water, rinsed and drained, broken into chunks

One 5-ounce can sliced water chestnuts, well drained

½ pound penne pasta (or other tubular pasta), cooked according to package directions

4 ounces Gruyère (or Swiss) cheese, grated

¼ cup chopped fresh parsley

1. Preheat the oven to 350°F. Spray a 9-by-13-inch casserole or baking dish with nonstick cooking spray.

2. In a large, deep skillet over medium-low heat, melt the butter. Add the mushrooms. Cook, stirring, for about 2 minutes.

3. In a bowl, whisk together the milk and flour and add to the pan. Add the broth and stir well.

4. Add the paprika, cayenne, Italian seasoning, nutmeg, and salt and black pepper to taste. Blend well.

5. Increase the heat to medium and cook until the sauce is thickened, about 3 minutes. Remove the pan from the heat.

6. Stir in the tuna and water chestnuts.

7. Add the cooked penne to the pan and blend well. Scrape the mixture into a baking dish.

8. Sprinkle the top with Gruyère cheese and parsley. Cover with foil, and bake in the oven for about 30 minutes. Remove the foil and bake for another 10 to 12 minutes. Let the casserole stand at room temperature for about 10 minutes before serving.

SHORT-CUT TIPS

SERVING TIP: Make smaller individual servings of this casserole by freezing in small plastic containers. First, line the containers with foil, add the casserole mixture, then freeze.

PLAN AHEAD: You can prepare this recipe up to the cheese and parsley additions, then freeze for cooking later.

STORAGE TIP: Once opened, unused canned water chestnuts should be transferred to a nonmetal container and covered with fresh water. If the water is changed every few days, they'll keep for up to 2 to 3 weeks.

FRESH ZUCCHINI AND TOASTED PINE NUTS PASTA

I think any dish with zucchini and pine nuts is really yummy, and this is a great recipe to make with leftover noodles. Try adding shredded carrots or yellow squash to this recipe for a variation. You may also use any pasta such as linguine, fettuccine, or angel hair instead of spaghetti.

MAKES 6 TO 8 SERVINGS

½ pound spaghetti, cooked according to package directions until al dente

2 small zucchini, shredded

¼ cup basil leaves, chopped

½ cup toasted pine nuts (see Time Saver opposite)

½ cup freshly grated Parmesan cheese

2 tablespoons olive oil, preferably extra-virgin

Salt and freshly ground black pepper

1. Place the hot, cooked noodles in a large mixing bowl.
2. Add the shredded zucchini and basil leaves. Toss together well.
3. Sprinkle the pine nuts and Parmesan cheese over the top and toss again.
4. Drizzle the olive oil over all. Season with the salt and pepper to taste, mix gently, and serve.

SHORT-CUT TIPS

TIME SAVER: Use your food processor to shred zucchini quickly.

TIME SAVER: Toast the pine nuts in a nonstick skillet over medium heat. Cook, stirring, until they're golden brown.

EASIER SHEPHERD'S PIE

Robert Reed, my television husband for five years on The Brady Bunch, *was the inspiration for this dish. Bob could do anything—he was a great gardener, cook, decorator, and pianist, as well as a superb actor and true friend. He once made me a beef-and-biscuit casserole topped with lots of cheese that was quite delicious. My recipe is probably a bit lighter than Bob's hearty one-dish meal, and closer to the classic shepherd's pie. If you want creamier mashed potatoes, make sure to heat the milk and broth together in the microwave before adding them to the potatoes.*

MAKES 4 TO 6 SERVINGS

FILLING

2 tablespoons olive oil

1 large onion, chopped

3 cloves garlic, chopped

2 pounds ground beef

2 carrots, thinly sliced

1 teaspoon dried rosemary

1 teaspoon dried thyme

Salt and freshly ground black pepper

One 14.5-ounce can whole tomatoes, chopped and partially drained

¾ cup beef, chicken, or vegetable broth

¼ cup dry white wine (or nonalcoholic wine or white grape juice)

TOPPING

2½ pounds potatoes, cut into chunks

½ bunch fresh parsley, chopped

½ bunch fresh basil, chopped

½ cup chicken broth

½ cup milk

Salt and freshly ground black pepper

1. To make the filling, in a large skillet over medium-high heat, heat the olive oil. Add the onion and garlic and cook, stirring, until the onions are translucent, 4 to 5 minutes.

2. Add the ground beef and cook, stirring, just until the meat is no longer pink, 4 to 5 minutes.

3. Stir in the carrot slices, rosemary, thyme, and salt and pepper to taste. Add the tomatoes, broth, and wine. Stir together well and cook for 5 to 6 minutes. Scrape the mixture into a shallow baking dish and set aside.

4. Preheat the oven to 375°F.

5. To make the topping, cook the potatoes in a large pot of salted water until they're softened, 15 to 20 minutes. Remove the potatoes to a colander to drain.

6. In a large bowl, with a fork, potato masher, or electric mixer on low speed, mash the potatoes. Add the parsley and the basil leaves. Stir well. Add the broth and the milk and blend until the mixture is creamy and smooth. Season to taste with the salt and pepper.

7. Spread the potatoes over the top of the meat mixture in the baking dish. Cover loosely with foil, and bake in the oven until the mixture is hot and bubbly inside, about 30 minutes. Remove the foil for the final 5 minutes of cooking time.

8. Let sit at room temperature for 10 minutes before serving.

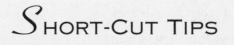

SHORT-CUT TIPS

SUBSTITUTION: Use fat-free broth and skim milk to create lower-fat potatoes.

MESS SAVER: For easy clean-up, line the casserole dish with foil before adding the filling.

SHOPPING TIP: For a real time saver, purchase premashed potatoes from the supermarket. They're often sold on a hot vegetable bar or can be found in the refrigerator or freezer sections ready to heat.

MUSHROOM-CHEESE WON TON RAVIOLI

If you really have a craving for something, nothing else will do, even if it takes a few extra minutes to make. So if it's ravioli you want and there's none on hand, you can easily create a substitute. Use won ton wrappers for the pasta! Then use your imagination to fill them with your favorite ingredients, such as precooked meat, chicken, and lobster, or cheeses, pesto, and nuts.

MAKES 4 SERVINGS

1 cup ricotta cheese

½ cup freshly grated Parmesan cheese

¼ cup chopped fresh basil leaves

1 teaspoon dried Italian seasoning

1 cup chopped fresh spinach

½ cup chopped fresh mushrooms (any domestic or wild, not dried)

Salt and freshly ground black pepper

1 package won ton wrappers

¼ cup water mixed with 2 teaspoons cornstarch

2 cups of favorite pasta sauce

Freshly grated Asiago or Parmesan cheese for topping

1. In a mixing bowl, combine the ricotta and Parmesan cheeses. Stir in the basil and Italian seasoning.

2. Add the chopped spinach and mushrooms. Blend together well. Season with the salt and black pepper to taste.

3. Cover the bowl and place it in the refrigerator for 30 minutes.

4. Place 12 to 16 won ton wrappers on a flat surface. Put 1 rounded tablespoon of the chilled mushroom-cheese filling in the center of each.

5. Dip your fingers into the water-cornstarch mixture and moisten the edges of each won ton. Top each moistened won ton with a second wrapper. Press the edges together firmly. Seal the edges with the tines of a fork. Repeat until all the filling is used.

6. Place the won ton ravioli in a single layer on a wax paper–lined baking sheet. Place them, uncovered, in the refrigerator to dry out somewhat, about 1 hour.

7. In a pan over medium-low heat, heat the pasta sauce. Don't let it come to a boil.

8. Add water to a deep skillet to about 3 inches deep. Add salt and bring to a boil over medium-high heat.

9. When the water comes to a gentle boil, add the ravioli, 3 to 4 at a time. Cook each batch for about 4 minutes. Remove the ravioli from the pan as they are cooked and set them aside to keep warm. Repeat until all are cooked.

10. Place 2 to 3 filled cooked ravioli on each dinner plate and top with the warm sauce. Sprinkle grated cheese over the top of each serving.

*S*HORT-CUT TIPS

MEASUREMENT SAVVY: One pound of fresh mushrooms equals about 6 cups of sliced.

SANITY SAVER: To clean fresh mushrooms before using, rinse them under cold running water and blot them dry with paper towels. Never fully immerse them, because they're very absorbent and will become mushy. You can also simply wipe them off with a damp paper towel. If you dip the paper towel in lemon juice, it helps to keep white mushrooms white until they're used. And don't peel mushrooms—this will cause them to lose their flavor.

DESSERTS

If you're trying to save time, preparing a complicated dessert is the last thing you want to do. But to a lot of people, the last part of the meal is the best, so don't deprive your friends or family of that pleasure.

To take the pressure off, keep some dessert staples in your pantry. By adding a few good-quality items, you can create a satisfying treat such as premium ice cream topped with fresh fruit, served in a beautiful water goblet, or just a store-bought plain cake with your favorite syrup drizzled over it. A plastic squeeze bottle for decoratively adding toppings is one of your best investments!

The sweet tooth belongs to the others in my family—I usually prefer fresh fruit to gooey desserts. But I do confess to being one of those people who loves fruitcake! I've frequently taken it on the road to have in a hotel room in the morning, when there's no time for a big breakfast.

Although I haven't the time to make such an elaborate dessert myself, I believe dessert time is whenever you feel like it, so the quick and easy recipes I'd like to share with you range from the lightest fruit tart to the richly satisfying Chocolate Mousse with Coffee Whipped Cream. Enjoy!

FREE-FORM APPLE-BERRY TART

Since I have fond memories of picking and selling berries as a kid, I always find fruit tarts a satisfying way to finish a meal. If you want this tart to be ready for you at the end of yours, assemble it at the same time that you prepare the rest of your food, then pop it in the oven about midway through eating. You'll be ready for each other right on time! If you don't have blueberries or raspberries, use any fruit or berries you enjoy to make free-form tarts—pears, apricots, peaches, raspberries, strawberries, or blackberries. They're all delicious!

MAKES 8 SERVINGS

1 premade piecrust (from the refrigerator section of the
   supermarket)

1 pound apples (Gala, Rome, Granny Smith,
   or Braeburn are all wonderful)

½ pint fresh or whole frozen blueberries

½ pint fresh or whole frozen raspberries

2 tablespoons lemon juice

3 tablespoons granulated sugar

1 teaspoon ground cinnamon

2 tablespoons all-purpose flour

1 tablespoon unsalted butter, chilled and cut
   into very small pieces

Powdered sugar to sprinkle on top of cooked tart

MINI:

QUICK AND DELICIOUS
RASPBERRY SORBET: **Puree
frozen raspberries in a
food processor, add
powdered sugar to taste,
and pour the mixture into
individual bowls. Place in
the freezer for about
30 minutes and serve!**

1. On a lightly floured surface, roll the piecrust dough out into a rough circle, about 14 inches in diameter. Place the dough circle on a baking sheet, cover with plastic wrap, and chill while you prepare the filling.

2. Core the apples and cut them into ¼-inch slices. You'll need about 2 cups of fruit. Place the slices in a glass mixing bowl.

3. Add the blueberries, raspberries, and lemon juice and toss gently.

4. Sprinkle 2 tablespoons of the sugar and the cinnamon over all and toss gently.

5. In a separate small bowl, mix together the remaining tablespoon of sugar and the flour. Set the mixture aside.

6. Preheat the oven to 400°F.

HOUSEHOLD HINT: To remove fruit and vegetable stains from your hands, rub with a paste of cornmeal and lemon juice (and salt if necessary), then rinse. This is effective for removing odors such as fish, onions, and garlic from hands as well.

*S*HORT-CUT TIPS

SERVING TIP: For a great buffet, make small individual tarts using this same recipe. Simply cut the rolled-out piecrust dough into 6 to 8 circles and divide the filling evenly among them, leaving a smaller 1-inch border. Bake as usual.

INGREDIENT SAVVY: When washing delicate berries such as blueberries and raspberries, place in a colander and rinse them under a gentle flow of cold water. Shake the colander gently and place the berries in a single layer on paper towels to dry.

TOOL TIP: If you don't have a rolling pin, take an empty wine bottle (remove the label), fill it with ice water, and close the top. Just roll out your pastry—the cold glass keeps it from sticking. When you're done, place the bottle back in the refrigerator to use again.

7. Remove the chilled piecrust from the refrigerator, take off the plastic wrap, and sprinkle the crust with the sugar-flour mixture. Leave a 2-inch border all around.

8. Arrange the fruit mixture evenly over the sugar-flour mixture, still leaving a 2-inch border. Fold the sides of the crust over the fruit, overlapping where necessary. Brush the folded areas of the crust with water and press them together. This creates the sides of the tart. The center area of the tart will be open. Scatter the butter pieces over the filling.

9. Bake the tart in the oven for about 30 minutes. Cover the outer edge of the crust with foil if it begins to get brown too quickly. The tart should be golden brown and bubbly, with the apples softened. Remove the tart from the oven and let it cool for about 10 minutes before serving.

10. When cooled down a bit, sift some powdered sugar over all. Cut the tart into wedges and serve.

CHOCOLATE BREAD PUDDING

I can't let my husband, John, near this dessert or there won't be any left for the rest of us! It's a speedy version of a favorite rich and creamy comfort food, and makes a great holiday treat. What a good way to use up leftover bread! You'll find the use of sourdough bread cubes a deliciously surprising addition to an old standby.

MAKES 6 TO 8 SERVINGS

1 cup semisweet chocolate chips (6 ounces)

1 cup heavy cream

½ cup firmly packed dark brown sugar

5 whole large eggs

½ cup (1 stick) unsalted butter, cut into pieces

2 teaspoons vanilla extract

2 tablespoons dark rum, or 1 teaspoon rum flavoring

4 cups sourdough bread cubes

1. Preheat the oven to 375°F. Spray a 2-quart casserole dish with nonstick cooking spray.

2. In a saucepan over low heat, melt together the semisweet chips and the cream. Stir often, until the mixture is smooth, being careful not to scorch the chocolate. Remove the pan from the heat, stir in the brown sugar, and let the chocolate cool slightly.

3. Place the eggs in a small bowl and beat gently. Pour ½ cup of the melted chocolate mixture into the eggs and whisk together gently. Add the egg mixture back into the saucepan, whisking as you add.

4. Add the butter pieces, vanilla, and rum. Blend well. Pour the mixture into a large mixing bowl.

5. Add the bread cubes and toss well. Scrape the mixture into the prepared dish. Place the casserole dish in a larger baking pan with about 1 inch of hot water in it.

6. Place in the oven and bake for about 30 minutes, until the pudding is set.

7. Serve hot or warm.

SHORT-CUT TIPS

SERVING TIP: Grated chocolate is a great garnish to sprinkle on bread pudding. Keep a block of chocolate in the freezer in a plastic freezer bag, and grate the block on a grater by pressing firmly. Or to make chocolate curls easily for garnishing, use a vegetable peeler on chocolate at room temperature.

INGREDIENT SAVVY: Store vanilla in a cool, dark place for up to a year. You can use vanilla to perk up a plain cup of coffee by adding a splash of it to the pot before you brew it, and create a great aroma in the kitchen.

FRUIT KEBABS

This dessert first seems like a cross between a Popsicle and a shish kebab. It can be served as a delicious side dish with grilled fish, steak, chicken, or pork, or at the end of the meal with a scoop of vanilla ice cream. If you don't have the fruits suggested here, try others like pitted cherries, mangoes, figs, oranges, strawberries, and apricots. If you're a little offbeat like I am, try pitted prunes—they're great with apricots.

MAKES 4 SERVINGS

3 ripe peaches or nectarines, cored and cut into wedges

2 ripe pears, cored and cut into wedges

½ ripe pineapple, peeled and cut into chunks (available precut in produce sections)

2 ripe but firm bananas, peeled and cut into 2-inch pieces

¼ cup brandy (or 1 teaspoon brandy flavoring plus 3 teaspoons apple juice; or ¼ cup peach syrup)

¼ cup orange-flavored or raspberry liqueur (or ¼ cup orange juice plus 2 teaspoons sugar)

2 tablespoons unsalted butter, melted

2 tablespoons sugar

> **MINI:**
>
> GRILLED WHOLE BANANAS: **Place bananas on a hot grill with the peel still on and cook, turning occasionally, for 5 to 8 minutes. The bananas will be soft and creamy, and wonderful served on top of hot waffles with real maple syrup!**

1. Preheat the grill or broiler.

2. Place all the fruit in a glass bowl.

3. In a microwave-safe measuring cup, whisk together the brandy, orange liqueur, melted butter, and sugar. Place it in the microwave and heat on high for 30 to 45 seconds, until the mixture is warm.

4. Thread the fruit alternately onto skewers and brush with the warm brandy mixture. Make 2 skewers per person.

5. Cook the skewers on the grill or on a broiler pan under the broiler for 3 to 4 minutes on each side. Brush again with the leftover brandy mixture as the skewers cook.

6. Serve fruit on the skewers with ice cream on the side for an appealing presentation.

SHORT-CUT TIPS

SUBSTITUTION: A dessert recipe that calls for brandy will work using peach syrup. So save the syrup from canned fruits by freezing it in an ice cube tray, then transfer the cubes to a plastic bag.

RECIPE RESCUE: Too much sugar in a recipe? Add a few drops of lemon juice or vinegar!

RECIPE RESCUE: To prevent wooden skewers from burning, soak them in a pan of water for a half hour before using.

SANITY SAVER: If using a whole fresh pineapple for this recipe, after you cut away the outer peel, slice it into 1-inch-thick rings. You can easily remove the hard inner core from each slice with a small round cookie cutter.

SANITY SAVER: When using measuring spoons, measure your dry ingredients first and then the liquid ingredients. That way, flour and sugar won't gum up in the cup.

QUICK CHOCOLATE MOUSSE WITH COFFEE WHIPPED CREAM

Here's an elegant, mouthwatering "no cook" dessert that you just mix up and refrigerate. If you don't even have the time to whip the cream, buy the real, prewhipped cream in an aerosol can. Then sprinkle the instant coffee over that and enjoy. If you're worried about not being able to fall asleep later, sprinkle the whipped cream with decaffeinated coffee! If you're worried about using uncooked eggs, to be safe, use the best-quality and freshest eggs possible.

MAKES 4 SERVINGS

⅔ cup semisweet chocolate chips or chopped chocolate, melted (4 ounces)

3 large eggs, separated

2 tablespoons dark rum (or 2 teaspoons almond extract)

½ cup heavy cream

1 teaspoon sugar

2 teaspoons instant coffee granules

Shaved chocolate for garnish

1. In a large bowl, combine the hot melted chocolate with the egg yolks and rum. Beat vigorously with an electric mixer. The mixture will be grainy and hard to mix at first, but will become smooth as you beat it.

2. In another bowl, with an electric mixer and clean beaters, beat the egg whites until soft peaks form. Fold into the chocolate mixture.

3. In another bowl, beat ¼ cup of the cream into soft peaks and fold it into the chocolate mixture.

4. Divide the mixture between 4 wineglasses or decorative serving bowls. Cover with plastic wrap and chill.

5. In a clean bowl, beat the remaining ¼ cup of cream with the sugar until stiff peaks form. Fold in the instant coffee granules.

6. To serve the mousse, add a dollop of whipped coffee cream to each glass and sprinkle with shaved chocolate.

SHORT-CUT TIPS

SERVING TIP: For fabulous chocolate "curls," spread melted chocolate evenly over the bottom of a cookie sheet. Let stand until the chocolate is set. Use a citrus zester to make the curls by pulling it through the chocolate!

SERVING TIP: For a great presentation with no fuss, serve this dessert in beautiful "chocolate bowls"! Just spread melted chocolate evenly over 8-inch circles of wax paper to within 1 inch of the edges. Place the circles, chocolate side up, over coffee mugs, turned upside down. Let them stand in the refrigerator to speed things up and, when set, peel the wax paper gently from the chocolate. Set the "bowls" on a flat surface and fill them with the mousse.

TIME SAVER: For great whipped cream, work with a chilled bowl, cream, and beaters. For great beaten egg whites, work with the whites, bowl, and beaters at room temperature.

SANITY SAVER: To avoid breaking the yolk when separating an egg, use 2 small custard cups. First crack the egg in one cup, then simply pour off the white part until the yolk is in one cup and the white in the other. Or buy an inexpensive egg separator from your local cook shop.

STORAGE TIP: Store whipped cream for later use by placing large drops of it on a cookie sheet and freezing them. Keep the "drops" in a tightly sealed plastic bag in the freezer to decorate pies and cakes.

FUN CHOCOLATE-DIPPED BITES

For impulse entertaining, this is a very "kid-friendly" dessert that even the youngest children can help make as well as eat. You'll probably want to melt the chocolate for them, then let them do the dipping. But don't be surprised when it's the grown-ups who make them disappear!

Melted semisweet chocolate (1 to 2 cups chips)

Melted white chocolate (1 to 2 cups chips)

Pretzels

Butter cookies

Strawberries, washed and well dried

Dried apricots

Bananas, peeled, cut into 4 equal pieces with a Popsicle stick inserted
       into each, then frozen

1. Cover cookie sheets or baking pans with wax paper. Set aside.

2. Stir each of the melted chocolates until smooth. Zap them in the microwave if they start to set up as you are using them.

3. Dip the pretzels halfway into the chocolates and lay them on the wax paper. Repeat with the butter cookies, berries, apricots, and frozen banana pieces. Dip each only halfway so guests can handle them without getting their fingers messy. You can double-dip if desired. Place the "bites" in the refrigerator until ready to serve them.

4. Arrange the "bites" in decorative patterns on serving platters.

SHORT-CUT TIPS

RECIPE RESCUE: When melting chocolate, make sure the bowl and spoon are *completely* dry. Even a little water can cause the chocolate to "seize" and become hard. To save it, add 1 teaspoon vegetable oil for each ounce of chocolate and stir until smooth. Do *not* use butter.

MESS SAVER: For easy clean-up, quickly melt chocolate by placing chips or chopped chocolate directly into a resealable plastic bag and placing the bag in a bowl of very hot water.

MESS SAVER: Fill a small plastic squeeze bottle with melted chocolate sauce to use for garnishing desserts or plates. You can store the leftover in the bottle in the refrigerator and place it in a pan of simmering water to remelt for future use.

SHOPPING TIP: There are some truly wonderful premade chocolate sauces on the market today. Look for these at your local supermarket to really save some time.

FRUIT BAKED IN PARCHMENT

If you don't have parchment for this recipe, aluminum foil will work. But when baking with foil, wrap foods with the shiny side out to keep them from overbrowning. To turn this easy recipe into a really decadent dessert, add a scoop of frozen yogurt or ice cream to the top of the fruit.

MAKES 4 SERVINGS

2 pears

2 Granny Smith apples (or other tart apple)

4 squares of parchment, approximately 12 by 12 inches

8 shortbread cookies

2 tablespoons unsalted butter, cut into pieces

Ground cinnamon

4 to 6 ounces crumbled blue cheese

2 tablespoons light or dark brown sugar

½ cup blackberry liqueur (or blackberry juice, currant juice, or peach nectar)

1. Preheat the oven to 400°F.

2. Peel, halve, and core the pears and apples. Cut into thick wedges.

3. Fold the parchment in half, creasing it down the middle.

4. Place an equal amount of apples and pears in the middle of one side of each sheet of parchment.

5. Crumble the cookies and sprinkle an equal amount over each mound of fruit.

6. Dot each with some of the butter pieces. Sprinkle some of the cinnamon to taste over all.

7. Scatter the crumbled blue cheese and some of the sugar over each.

8. Drizzle all four with the liqueur.

9. Fold the other half of the parchment sheet over the fruit and fold the edges together to create a "package." Use toothpicks to pin the edges together if necessary.

10. Place the fruit packages on a baking sheet and bake in the oven for 10 to 12 minutes. Serve the fruit on dessert plates with the parchment cut open.

SHORT-CUT TIPS

SUBSTITUTION: Instead of using the topping called for in this recipe, mix together ¼ cup ground almonds, ¼ cup brown sugar, and ¼ cup chopped pecans. Sprinkle it over the top of the fruit to create a nutty crumble topping when baked.

STORAGE TIP: Ground spices such as cinnamon lose their flavor and aroma quickly, so purchase small quantities, then store them in airtight containers in a cool, dark place, *never* over a hot stove.

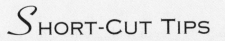

PAN-FRIED FRUIT

When we were growing up, I always enjoyed fried green apples. So for an interesting and colorful dessert, I tried this combination of quick-cooking ingredients. The addition of yellow bell pepper to this recipe might seem a bit unusual, but it's actually very sweet, and when cooked, complements the other fruit. I think it's a great ending to a meal!

MAKES 4 TO 6 SERVINGS

1 tablespoon unsalted butter

2 pears, halved, cored, and sliced about ½ inch thick

2 tart red apples, halved, cored, and sliced

½ medium yellow bell pepper, cut into slivers

½ cup chopped dried peaches

¼ cup apple juice

¼ cup maple syrup

Splash of balsamic vinegar

1. In a nonstick skillet over medium-high heat, melt the butter.

2. When the butter is melted, add the pears, apples, bell pepper, and dried peaches. Cook, stirring often, for about 3 minutes.

3. Pour in the apple juice and maple syrup. Stir well. Reduce the heat to medium and cook, stirring often, until the fruit begins to soften, 6 to 8 minutes. Add a bit of water if the liquid cooks off too quickly.

4. Remove the pan from the heat. Stir well and add a splash of vinegar. Stir again and serve.

SHORT-CUT TIPS

SERVING TIP: This pan-fried fruit recipe is delicious when chilled.

SUBSTITUTION: If you don't like the flavor of maple syrup, when preparing this recipe, try using the same amount of currant jelly or apricot preserves instead.

SANITY SAVER: If bell peppers "repeat" on you, remove the offending agent, which is in the skin, by peeling it with a vegetable peeler.

DARK CHERRY CLAFOUTI

You can use any number of your favorite fruits to make a classic French clafouti. Try it with peaches, nectarines, pears, fresh cherries, or frozen whole berries. I save some time by using canned, pitted cherries. This dessert is a wonderful ending to a steak dinner.

M A K E S 6 S E R V I N G S

⅓ cup all-purpose flour

½ teaspoon baking powder

1 teaspoon ground cinnamon

3 large eggs

¼ cup milk

¼ cup granulated sugar

Two 16-ounce cans pitted cherries, drained

Powdered sugar

1. Preheat the oven to 400°F. Spray a 10-inch pie plate with nonstick cooking spray.

2. In a mixing bowl, blend together the flour, baking powder, and ground cinnamon.

3. In another bowl, lightly beat the eggs. Whisk the milk and granulated sugar into the eggs.

4. Combine the egg mixture and the flour mixture and blend well.

5. Scatter the drained cherries evenly over the bottom of the pie plate.

6. Pour the egg-flour mixture over the fruit. Bake in the oven for about

30 minutes or until the center is set. Remove the plate from the oven and serve hot or warm.

7. To garnish, sprinkle powdered sugar over the top of each serving.

---

*S*HORT-CUT TIPS

SUBSTITUTION: If you don't have baking powder, you can make your own. For the equivalent of 1 teaspoon of baking powder, mix ¼ teaspoon baking soda plus ½ teaspoon cream of tartar.

SUBSTITUTION: If you don't have powdered sugar, make your own. Blend 1 cup granulated sugar plus 1 tablespoon cornstarch in a blender on medium for 2 minutes. If you use it often, keep a shaker with a mesh top filled with powdered sugar to dust on the tops of desserts. Put a few grains of rice in the shaker to absorb moisture.

SANITY SAVERS: Baking powder loses its effectiveness over time. To test, put ½ teaspoon of powder into ¼ cup of hot tap water. If it bubbles, it's still fresh. If not, discard it.

Never dip a wet spoon into the baking powder can. The excess moisture can cause baking powder to deteriorate quickly.

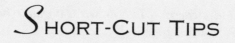

BERRY, BERRY CORNMEAL CAKES

My daughter Barbara and I have similar tastes when it comes to dessert—we like dense textures, which is why I love this recipe. This is good to make when local fresh berries are in season, and you can use any combination you enjoy. The cornmeal gives the shortcake its thick texture—and the nutty flavor complements the tangy sweetness of the fruit. It's pretty served with the vanilla yogurt, and perfect to serve with a cup of tea.

MAKES 4 TO 6 SERVINGS

½ pint *each* fresh raspberries and blackberries (whole frozen if fresh
    aren't available)

2 tablespoons light or dark brown sugar

1½ cups all-purpose flour

½ cup fine yellow cornmeal

¼ cup granulated sugar

2 teaspoons baking soda

1 teaspoon cream of tartar

½ teaspoon salt

½ cup (1 stick) cold unsalted butter, cut into small pieces

1 cup plain yogurt

Milk for glaze

1 cup vanilla-flavored yogurt

1. In a glass mixing bowl, combine the raspberries, blackberries, and
   brown sugar. Mix together with a fork, crushing some of the berries as
   you mix. Leave some whole. Cover the bowl with plastic wrap and chill
   until ready to use.

2. Preheat the oven to 425°F.

3. In a bowl, whisk together the flour, cornmeal, granulated sugar, baking
   soda, cream of tartar, and salt.

4. Cut the cold butter pieces into the flour mixture, using a pastry blender
   or 2 knives as you would when making biscuits, until the mixture
   resembles coarse crumbs.

5. Make a "well" in the center of the flour mixture and add the plain
   yogurt. Stir until a soft dough forms.

6. Turn the mixture out onto a lightly floured surface and knead it to
   form a biscuitlike dough. With floured hands, pat the dough out to
   about ½ inch thick.

7. Using a 3-inch round cookie cutter, cut the dough into circles. Gather the scraps of dough, pat them out again, and cut more circles until all the dough is used.

8. Place the circles of dough on an ungreased baking sheet and brush the top of each with some milk.

9. Bake in the oven for about 20 minutes, until the cakes are golden brown. Remove them from the oven and cool slightly on a cooling rack.

10. To serve, place 1 or 2 cakes on each dessert plate. Top with the chilled berry mixture and add a dollop of vanilla yogurt.

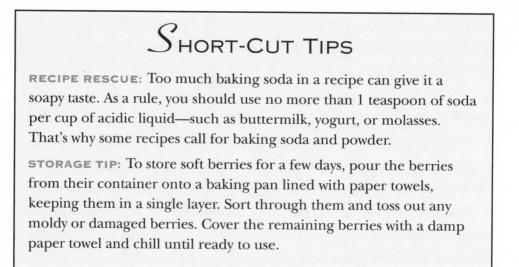

SHORT-CUT TIPS

RECIPE RESCUE: Too much baking soda in a recipe can give it a soapy taste. As a rule, you should use no more than 1 teaspoon of soda per cup of acidic liquid—such as buttermilk, yogurt, or molasses. That's why some recipes call for baking soda and powder.

STORAGE TIP: To store soft berries for a few days, pour the berries from their container onto a baking pan lined with paper towels, keeping them in a single layer. Sort through them and toss out any moldy or damaged berries. Cover the remaining berries with a damp paper towel and chill until ready to use.

BUTTERMILK WAFFLE STRAWBERRY SHORTCAKES

Waffles always meant breakfast to me until I tried this dessert at a friend's party. It's a light combination of tart and sweet, which I now like to serve for brunch as well as dinner. The balsamic vinegar gives it a real kick, and it perks up the crunchy waffle. Since it takes no time to prepare, it's a treat any time you make it.

MAKES 4 SERVINGS

1 pint strawberries, washed, hulled, and thickly sliced

¼ cup granulated sugar

3 tablespoons balsamic vinegar

1 cup sour cream

1 tablespoon lemon juice

2 tablespoons light or dark brown sugar, or to taste

4 frozen buttermilk waffles

1. Place the berries in a glass mixing bowl and sprinkle with the granulated sugar. Stir, slightly mashing the fruit, until the sugar is dissolved.

2. Add the balsamic vinegar and stir to blend. Cover with plastic wrap and chill until ready to serve.

3. In a bowl, combine the sour cream, lemon juice, and brown sugar. Mix well and adjust the sugar to taste.

4. To serve, toast the frozen waffles in the toaster until golden brown and crispy. Place 1 on each dessert plate.

5. Top each waffle with an equal amount of the fruit and juice mixture, and add a dollop of the sour cream mixture. Serve immediately.

---

*S*HORT-CUT TIPS

SUBSTITUTE: Instead of regular waffles, use frozen Belgian waffles for this recipe. Also try it with frozen French toast. Substitute or add banana slices to the strawberries. Delicious!

SANITY SAVER: To break up hardened brown sugar, place it in a blender and give it a quick zap. It will be much easier to mix into recipes. You can also soften "hard as a rock" brown sugar by placing a slice of soft bread or half an apple in the package and closing it tightly. It will be soft in a few hours.

SANITY SAVER: To keep granulated sugar from lumping, place a couple of saltines in the container with the sugar and cover it tightly.

ZESTY BROWNIES

Here's a way to spice up America's most popular bar cookie—the brownie. To create a soft, moist, chewy brownie, take care to cook just until the batter has set. If you like a drier, cakelike brownie, cook it for another 5 to 10 minutes. The unusual addition of cayenne pepper (also called red pepper) doesn't make the brownies hot, but it gives them a very gentle, spicy bite. You'll want to take a very big bite of yours!

MAKES 16 BARS (APPROXIMATELY, DEPENDING ON DESIRED SIZE)

½ cup (1 stick) unsalted butter, softened

2 cups semisweet chocolate chips (12 ounces)

1½ cups sugar

1 teaspoon vanilla extract

1½ cups all-purpose flour

½ teaspoon baking powder

½ teaspoon salt

½ teaspoon cayenne pepper

3 large eggs

1 cup chopped toasted pecans (page 44—optional)

1. Preheat the oven to 350°F. Lightly grease an 8-inch square baking pan with shortening.

2. Place the butter and the chocolate chips in a glass mixing bowl and microwave them on high for 1-minute intervals until the mixture is melted. Stir until smooth.

3. Stir in the sugar and the vanilla extract until well mixed.

4. In another bowl, whisk together the flour, baking powder, salt, and cayenne pepper.

5. Add the flour mixture to the melted chocolate and stir to combine.

6. Add the eggs and stir until well incorporated.

7. Stir in ½ cup of the pecans and blend well. Scrape the mixture into the prepared pan.

8. Sprinkle the top with the remaining ½ cup of pecans. Bake in the oven for about 30 minutes or until set. Be careful not to overcook.

9. Remove the pan from the oven and place it on a wire cooling rack to cool before cutting. Cut the brownies into squares. Serve warm or at room temperature.

*S*HORT-CUT TIPS

SERVING TIP: For a grander or more fun presentation, try cutting brownies into decorative shapes. Cut them on the diagonal to form diamonds, or use shaped cookie cutters for special occasions. Cut them into very small, bite-sized cubes for parties.

MEASUREMENT SAVVY: A 5-pound bag of all-purpose flour, unsifted, equals 17½ cups of flour. To properly measure flour, stir the flour in the bag with a fork. Scoop out the flour with a dry measure—one which is the exact size of the measure you want (not a whole cup glass measure). Then "level" it with the back of a knife, over the bag.

RECIPE RESCUE: If the edges of your brownie mixture have burned, you can save some of it by scooping out the interior or top, which is still somewhat moist, and putting it in parfait dishes. Top with whipping cream and serve!

SANITY SAVER: Grease your baking pan with shortening instead of butter, which sometimes browns too quickly. Nonstick sprays will cause foods to stick at times.

MESS SAVER: Line the baking pan with foil before adding the batter, then grease it as usual. When the brownies are baked, they can be easily lifted from the pan by the foil edges. Easy clean-up!

CHOCOLATE FUDGE
APPLESAUCE CAKE

Here's a super-fast dessert for the cake lovers in your family, since just about all the ingredients come in a package or jar—the cake mix, nuts, chips, and applesauce. The applesauce is a low-fat substitute for oil and creates a nice, moist cake. If you're not watching your calorie intake and you'd like your cake with a topping, you can quickly create some fudge icing. Just melt together 1 cup semisweet chocolate chips and ¼ cup heavy cream, and stir until smooth. Pour the mixture into a resealable bag, snip off a corner, and squeeze it decoratively over the cake.

MAKES ABOUT 20 SERVINGS

One 18.5-ounce package devil's food cake mix (your favorite brand)

2 cups applesauce

1 large egg

½ cup your favorite chopped nuts (pecans, walnuts, almonds, or
   hazelnuts)

½ cup semisweet chocolate chips

1. Preheat the oven to 350°F. Grease and flour a 12-cup Bundt pan or 10-inch tube pan.

2. In a mixing bowl, using an electric mixer on low speed, combine the cake mix, applesauce, and egg until the mix is moistened. Increase the speed to medium and beat for 2 more minutes.

3. Add the nuts and chocolate chips and blend well.

4. Scrape the batter into the prepared pan and smooth the top. Bake in the oven for about 45 minutes, or until a toothpick inserted into the

center of the cake comes out clean. Cool the cake on a rack for about 10 minutes. Invert it onto a serving plate. Serve warm or at room temperature.

SHORT-CUT TIPS

RECIPE RESCUE: If you overbake a cake or it's too dry, make holes through the cake with a skewer (or a chopstick), then drizzle with your favorite liqueur or syrup to moisten it. Let the cake sit for a while to absorb the liquid before serving.

SANITY SAVER: To keep a mixing bowl steady or from moving on a counter while you work with it, place a damp cloth underneath it.

SANITY SAVER: If your applesauce is too sweet, add a teaspoon of lemon juice. If it's not sweet enough, add some honey, maple syrup, or sugar.

STORAGE TIP: Keep chocolate chips in a cool dry place in a jar with a tight-fitting lid.

INDEX